GLOBAL RECESSION – CAUSES, IMPACTS AND REMEDIES

FINANCIAL REGULATORY REFORM

GLOBAL RECESSION – CAUSES, IMPACTS AND REMEDIES

Recessions: Prospects and Developments
Nerea M. Pérez and June A. Ortega (Editors)
2009. ISBN: 978-1-60456-866-0

Financial Crisis in America
Raymund T. Ovanhouser (Editor)
2009. ISBN: 978-1-60692-191-3

Economic Crises as a Result of Distrust
Emilio Gullini (Editor)
2010. ISBN: 978-1-60741-355-4

Financial Regulatory Reform
Stephen E. Moyer (Editor)
2010. ISBN: 978-1-60741-567-1

Economic Stimulus: Plans, Risks and Outlook
Samuel P. Turner (Editor)
2010. ISBN: 978-1-60741-516-9

Financial Markets and the Global Recession
Benjamin Naas and Joachim Lysne (Editors)
2010. ISBN: 978-1-60741-921-1

Assessing Treasury's Strategy - Six Months of TARP
Jarod R. Acosto (Editor)
2010. ISBN: 978-1-60876-139-5

Reassessing TARP: Second Report from the Special Inspector General
George T. Bernhardt (Editor)
2010. ISBN: 978-1-60741-965-5
2010. ISBN: 978-1-61668-378-8 (E-book)

Financial Crisis in the Global Bubble Economy
Akinori Tomohara and Molly Sherlock (Editors)
2010. ISBN: 978-1-61668-339-9

GLOBAL RECESSION – CAUSES, IMPACTS AND REMEDIES

FINANCIAL REGULATORY REFORM

STEPHEN E. MOYER
EDITOR

Nova Science Publishers, Inc.
New York

LIBRARY OF CONGRESS CATALOGING-IN-PUBLICATION DATA

Financial regulatory reform / editor, Stephen E. Moyer.
p. cm.
Includes index.
ISBN 978-1-60741-567-1 (hbk.)
1. Finance--Government policy--United States. 2. Financial services industry--Government policy--United States. 3. Banks and banking--State supervision--United States. I. Moyer, Stephen E.
HG181.F643453 2009
332.10973--dc22

2009041002

Published by Nova Science Publishers, Inc. ✣ New York

CONTENTS

PREFACE

The current U.S. financial regulatory system has relied on a fragmented and complex arrangement of federal and state regulators - put into place over the past 150 years - that has not kept pace with major developments in financial markets and products in recent decades. As the nation finds itself in the midst of one of the worst financial crisis ever, it has become apparent that the regulatory system is ill-suited to meet the nation's needs in the 21st century. This book examines several key changes in financial markets and products in recent decades and highlights significant limitations and gaps in the existing regulatory system. In addition, the authors of this book identify eight specific areas most urgently in need of reform and make recommendations for the future. This book consists of public documents which have been located, gathered, combined, reformatted, and enhanced with a subject index, selectively edited and bound to provide easy access.

Chapter 1 - This chapter is edited and excerpted testimony Gene L. Dodaro before the Committee on Banking, Housing and Urban Affairs, U.S. Senate, dated February 4, 2009.

Chapter 2 - 1. Lessons from the Past - Financial crises are not new. As early as 1792, during the presidency of George Washington, the nation suffered a severe panic that froze credit and nearly brought the young economy to its knees. Over the next 140 years, financial crises struck on a regular basis—in 1797, 1819, 1837, 1857, 1873, 1893–96, 1907, and 1929–33—roughly every fifteen to twenty years.

But as the United States emerged from the Great Depression, something remarkable happened: the crises stopped. New financial regulation—including federal deposit insurance, securities regulation, and banking supervision—effectively protected the system from devastating outbreaks. Economic growth returned, but recurrent financial crises did not. In time, a financial crisis was seen as a ghost of the past.

After fifty years without a financial crisis—the longest such stretch in the nation's history— financial firms and policy makers began to see regulation as a barrier to efficient functioning of the capital markets rather than a necessary precondition for success.

This change in attitude had unfortunate consequences. As financial markets grew and globalized, often with breathtaking speed, the U.S. regulatory system could have benefited from smart changes. But deregulation and the growth of unregulated, parallel shadow markets were accompanied by the nearly unrestricted marketing of increasingly complex consumer financial products that multiplied risk at every stratum of the economy, from the family level to the global level. The result proved disastrous. The first warning followed deregulation of the thrifts, when the country suffered the savings and loan crisis in the 1980s. A second warning came in 1998 when a crisis was only narrowly averted following the failure of a large unregulated hedge fund. The near financial panic of 2002, brought on by corporate accounting and governance failures, sounded a third warning.

The United States now faces its worst financial crisis since the Great Depression. It is critical that the lessons of that crisis be studied to restore a proper balance between free markets and the regulatory framework necessary to ensure the operation of those markets to protect the economy, honest market participants, and the public.

2. Shortcomings of the Present - The current crisis should come as no surprise. The present regulatory system has failed to effectively manage risk, require sufficient transparency, and ensure fair dealings.

Financial markets are inherently volatile and prone to extremes. The government has a critical role to play in helping to manage both public and private risk. Without clear and effective rules in place, productive financial activity can degenerate into unproductive gambling, while sophisticated financial transactions, as well as more ordinary consumer credit transactions, can give way to swindles and fraud.

A well-regulated financial system serves a key public purpose: if it has the power and if its leaders have the will to use that power, it channels savings and investment into productive economic activity and helps prevent financial contagion. Like the management of any complex hazard, financial regulation should not rely on a single magic bullet, but instead should employ an array of related measures for managing various elements of risk. The advent of the automobile brought enormous benefits but also considerable risks to drivers, passengers, and pedestrians. The solution was not to prohibit driving, but rather to manage the risks through reasonable speed limits, better road construction, safer sidewalks, required safety devices (seatbelts, airbags, children's car seats, antilock breaks), mandatory automobile insurance, and so on. The same holds true in the financial sector.

In recent years, however, the regulatory system not only failed to manage risk, it also failed to require disclosure of risk through sufficient transparency. American financial markets are profoundly dependent upon transparency. After all, the fundamental risk/reward corollary depends on the ability of market participants to have confidence in their ability to accurately judge risk.

Markets have become opaque in multiple ways. Some markets, such as hedge funds and credit default swaps, provide virtually no information. Even so, disclosure alone does not always provide genuine transparency. Market participants must have useful, relevant information delivered in an appropriate, timely manner. Recent market occurrences involving off-balance-sheet entities and complex financial instruments reveal the lack of transparency resulting from the wrong information disclosed at the wrong time and in the wrong manner. Mortgage documentation suffers from a similar problem, with reams of paper thrust at borrowers at closing, far too late for any borrower to make a well-informed decision. Just as markets and financial products evolve, so too must efforts to provide understanding through genuine transparency.

To compound the problem associated with uncontained and opaque risks, the current regulatory framework has failed to ensure fair dealings. Unfair dealing can be blatant, such as outright deception or fraud, but unfairness can also be much more subtle, as when parties are unfairly matched. Individuals have limited time and expertise to master complex financial dealings. If one party to a transaction has significantly more resources, time, sophistication or experience, other parties are at a fundamental disadvantage. The regulatory system should take appropriate steps to level the playing field.

Unfair dealings affect not only the specific transaction participants, but extend across entire markets, neighborhoods, socioeconomic groups, and whole industries. Even when only a limited number of families in one neighborhood have been the direct victims of a predatory lender, the entire neighborhood and even the larger community will suffer very real consequences from the resulting foreclosures. As those consequences spread, the entire financial system can be affected as well. More importantly, unfairness, or even the perception of unfairness, causes a loss of confidence in the marketplace. It becomes all the more critical for regulators to ensure fairness through meaningful disclosure, consumer protection measures, stronger enforcement, and other measures. Fair dealings provide credibility to businesses and satisfaction to consumers.

In tailoring regulatory responses to these and other problems, the goal should always be to strike a reasonable balance between the costs of regulation and its benefits. Just as speed limits are more stringent on busy city streets than on open highways, financial regulation should be strictest where the threats—especially the threats to other citizens—are greatest, and it should be more moderate elsewhere.

3. Recommendations for the Future - Modern financial regulation can provide consumers and investors with adequate information for making sound financial decisions and can protect them from being misled or defrauded, especially in complex financial transactions. Better regulation can reduce conflicts of interest and help manage moral hazard, particularly by limiting incentives for excessive risk taking stemming from often implicit government guaranties. By limiting risk taking in key parts of the financial sector, regulation can reduce systemic threats to the broader financial system and the economy as a whole. Ultimately, financial regulation embodies good risk management, transparency, and fairness.

Had regulators given adequate attention to even one of the three key areas of risk management, transparency and fairness, we might have averted the worst aspects of the current crisis.

1. Risk management should have been addressed through better oversight of systemic risks. If companies that are now deemed "too big to fail" had been better regulated, either to diminish their systemic impact or to curtail the risks they took, then these companies could have been allowed to fail or to reorganize without taxpayer bailouts. The creation of any new implicit government guarantee of high-risk business activities could have been avoided.
2. Transparency should have been addressed though better, more accurate credit ratings. If companies issuing high-risk credit instruments had not been able to obtain AAA ratings from the private credit rating agencies, then pension funds, financial institutions, state and local municipalities, and others that relied on those ratings would not have been misled into making dangerous investments.
3. Fairness should have been addressed though better regulation of consumer financial products. If the excesses in mortgage lending had been curbed by even the most minimal consumer protection laws, the loans that were fed into the mortgage backed securities would have been

choked off at the source, and there would have been no "toxic assets" to threaten the global economy.

While the current crisis had many causes, it was not unforeseeable. Correcting the mistakes that fueled this crisis is within reach. The challenge now is to develop a new set of rules for a new financial system.

The Panel has identified eight specific areas most urgently in need of reform:

1. Identify and regulate financial institutions that pose systemic risk.
2. Limit excessive leverage in American financial institutions.
3. Increase supervision of the shadow financial system.
4. Create a new system for federal and state regulation of mortgages and other consumer credit products.
5. Create executive pay structures that discourage excessive risk taking.
6. Reform the credit rating system.
7. Make establishing a global financial regulatory floor a U.S. diplomatic priority.
8. Plan for the next crisis.

While these are the most pressing reform recommendations, many other issues merit further study, the results of which the Panel will present in future reports. Despite the magnitude of the task, the central message is clear: through modernized regulation, we can dramatically reduce the risk of crises and swindles while preserving the key benefits of a vibrant financial system

Americans have paid dearly for this latest crisis. Lost jobs, failed businesses, foreclosed homes, and sharply cut retirement savings have touched people all across the county. Now every citizen—even the most prudent—is called on to assume trillions of dollars in liabilities spent to try to repair a broken system. The costs of regulatory failure and the urgency of regulatory reform could not be clearer.

In: Financial Regulatory Reform
Editors: Stephen E. Moyer

ISBN: 978-1-60741-567-1

Chapter 1

FINANCIAL REGULATION: A FRAMEWORK FOR CRAFTING AND ASSESSING PROPOSALS TO MODERNIZE THE OUTDATED U.S. FINANCIAL REGULATORY SYSTEM

Government Accountability Office

Mr. Chairman and Members of the Committee:

I am pleased to be here today to discuss our January 8, 2009, report that provides a framework for modernizing the outdated U.S. financial regulatory system.[1] We prepared this work under the authority of the Comptroller General to help policymakers weigh various regulatory reform proposals and consider ways in which the current regulatory system could be made more effective and efficient. My statement today is based on our report, which (1) describes how regulation has evolved in banking, securities, thrifts, credit unions, futures, insurance, secondary mortgage markets and other important areas; (2) describes several key changes in financial markets and products in recent decades that have highlighted significant limitations and gaps in the existing regulatory system; and (3) presents an evaluation framework that can be used by Congress and others to shape potential regulatory reform efforts. On January 22, we released an update to our biennial High-Risk Series, which described high-risk areas in federal programs, including focusing on the need for broad-based transformations to address major economy, efficiency, or effectiveness challenges. Based on recent economic events and our past work on financial regulatory reform, we added the need to modernize the outdated U.S. financial regulatory system as a new high-risk area this year.[2]

To do this work, we synthesized existing GAO work and other studies and met with representatives of financial regulatory agencies, industry associations, consumer advocacy organizations, and others. The work upon which the report is based was conducted in accordance with generally accepted government auditing standards. Those standards require that we plan and perform the audit to obtain sufficient, appropriate evidence to provide a reasonable basis for our findings and conclusions based on our audit objectives. We believe that the evidence obtained provides a reasonable basis for our findings and conclusions based on our audit objectives. This work was conducted between April 2008 and December 2008.

The report was enhanced by input from representatives of 29 agencies and other organizations, including federal and state financial regulatory agencies, consumer advocacy groups, and financial service industry trade associations, who reviewed and commented on a draft of the report prior to its release. A list of organizations that reviewed the draft report is included at the end of my statement. In general, reviewers commented that the report represented an important and thorough review of the issues related to regulatory reform.

SUMMARY

The current U.S. financial regulatory system has relied on a fragmented and complex arrangement of federal and state regulators—put into place over the past 150 years—that has not kept pace with major developments in financial markets and products in recent decades. Today, almost a dozen federal regulatory agencies, numerous self-regulatory organizations, and hundreds of state financial regulatory agencies share responsibility for overseeing the financial services industry. As the nation finds itself in the midst of one of the worst financial crises ever, it has become apparent that the regulatory system is ill-suited to meet the nation's needs in the 21st century.

Several key changes in financial markets and products in recent decades have highlighted significant limitations and gaps in the existing regulatory system.

- First, regulators have struggled, and often failed, to mitigate the systemic risks posed by large and interconnected financial conglomerates and to ensure they adequately manage their risks.
- Second, regulators have had to address problems in financial markets resulting from the activities of large and sometimes less-regulated market participants—such as nonbank mortgage lenders, hedge funds, and credit rating agencies—some of which play significant roles in today's financial markets.
- Third, the increasing prevalence of new and more complex investment products has challenged regulators and investors, and consumers have faced difficulty understanding new and increasingly complex retail mortgage and credit products.
- Fourth, standard setters for accounting and financial regulators have faced growing challenges in ensuring that accounting and audit standards appropriately respond to financial market developments, and in addressing challenges arising from the global convergence of accounting and auditing standards.
- Finally, as financial markets have become increasingly global, the current fragmented U.S. regulatory structure has complicated some efforts to coordinate internationally with other regulators.

These significant developments have outpaced a fragmented and outdated regulatory structure, and, as a result, significant reforms to the U.S. regulatory system are critically and urgently needed. The current system has significant weaknesses that, if not addressed, will continue to expose the nation's financial system to serious risks. Our report offers a framework for crafting and evaluating regulatory reform proposals consisting of nine characteristics that should be reflected in any new regulatory system. By applying the elements of the framework, the relative strengths and weaknesses of any reform proposal should be better revealed, and policymakers should be able to focus on identifying tradeoffs and balancing competing goals. Similarly, the framework could be used to craft proposals, or to identify aspects to be added to existing proposals to make them more effective and appropriate for addressing the limitations of the current system..

As the administration and Congress continue to take actions to address the immediate financial crisis, determining how to create a regulatory system that reflects new market realities is a key step to reducing the likelihood that the United States will experience another financial crisis similar to the current one.

Table 1. Framework for Crafting and Evaluating Regulatory Reform Proposals

Characteristic	Description
• Clearly defined regulatory goals	Goals should be clearly articulated and relevant, so that regulators can effectively carry out their missions and be held accountable. Key issues include considering the benefits of reexamining the goals of financial regulation to gain needed consensus and making explicit a set of updated comprehensive and cohesive goals that reflect today's environment.
• Appropriately comprehensive	Financial regulations should cover all activities that pose risks or are otherwise important to meeting regulatory goals and should ensure that appropriate determinations are made about how extensive such regulations should be, considering that some activities may require less regulation than others. Key issues include identifying risk-based criteria, such as a product's or institution's potential to create systemic problems, for determining the appropriate level of oversight for financial activities and institutions, including closing gaps that contributed to the current crisis.
• Systemwide focus	Mechanisms should be included for identifying, monitoring, and managing risks to the financial system regardless of the source of the risk. Given that no regulator is currently tasked with this, key issues include determining how to effectively monitor market developments to identify potential risks; the degree, if any, to which regulatory intervention might be required; and who should hold such responsibilities.
• Flexible and adaptable	A regulatory system that is flexible and forward looking allows regulators to readily adapt to market innovations and changes. Key issues include identifying and acting on emerging risks in a timely way without hindering innovation.
• Efficient and effective	Effective and efficient oversight should be developed, including eliminating overlapping federal regulatory missions where appropriate, and minimizing regulatory burden without sacrificing effective oversight. Any changes to the system should be continually focused on improving the effectiveness of the financial regulatory system. Key issues include determining opportunities for consolidation given the large number of overlapping participants now, identifying the appropriate role of states and self-regulation, and ensuring a smooth transition to any new system.

Table 1. (Continued)

Characteristic	Description
• Consistent consumer and investor protection	Consumer and investor protection should be included as part of the regulatory mission to ensure that market participants receive consistent, useful information, as well as legal protections for similar financial products and services, including disclosures, sales practice standards, and suitability requirements. Key issues include determining what amount, if any, of consolidation of responsibility may be necessary to streamline consumer protection activities across the financial services industry.
• Regulators provided with independence, prominence, authority, and accountability	Regulators should have independence from inappropriate influence, as well as prominence and authority to carry out and enforce statutory missions, and be clearly accountable for meeting regulatory goals. With regulators with varying levels of prominence and funding schemes now, key issues include how to appropriately structure and fund agencies to ensure that each one's structure sufficiently achieves these characteristics.
• Consistent financial oversight	Similar institutions, products, risks, and services should be subject to consistent regulation, oversight, and transparency, which should help minimize negative competitive outcomes while harmonizing oversight, both within the United States and internationally. Key issues include identifying activities that pose similar risks, and streamlining regulatory activities to achieve consistency.
• Minimal taxpayer exposure	A regulatory system should foster financial markets that are resilient enough to absorb failures and thereby limit the need for federal intervention and limit taxpayers' exposure to financial risk. Key issues include identifying safeguards to prevent systemic crises and minimizing moral hazard.

TODAY'S FINANCIAL REGULATORY SYSTEM WAS BUILT OVER THE COURSE OF MORE THAN A CENTURY, LARGELY IN RESPONSE TO CRISES OR MARKET DEVELOPMENTS

As a result of 150 years of changes in financial regulation in the United States, the regulatory system has become complex and fragmented. Today, responsibilities for overseeing the financial services industry are shared among almost a dozen federal banking, securities, futures, and other regulatory agencies, numerous self-regulatory organizations, and hundreds of state financial regulatory agencies. In particular, five federal agencies— including the Federal Deposit Insurance Corporation, the Federal Reserve, the Office of the Comptroller of the Currency, the Office of Thrift Supervision, and the National Credit Union Administration—and multiple state agencies oversee depository institutions. Securities activities are overseen by the Securities and Exchange Commission and state government entities, as well as by private sector organizations performing self-regulatory functions. Futures trading is overseen by the Commodity Futures Trading Commission and also by industry self-regulatory organizations. Insurance activities are primarily regulated at the state level with little federal involvement. Other federal regulators also play important roles in the financial regulatory system, such as the Public Company Accounting Oversight Board, which oversees the activities of public accounting firms, and the Federal Trade Commission, which acts as the primary federal agency responsible for enforcing compliance with federal consumer protection laws for financial institutions, such as finance companies, which are not overseen by another financial regulator.

Much of this structure has developed as the result of statutory and regulatory changes that were often implemented in response to financial crises or significant developments in the financial services sector. For example, the Federal Reserve System was created in 1913 in response to financial panics and instability around the turn of the century, and much of the remaining structure for bank and securities regulation was created as the result of the Great Depression turmoil of the 1920s and 1930s. Changes in the types of financial activities permitted for depository institutions and their affiliates have also shaped the financial regulatory system over time. For example, under the Glass-Steagall provisions of the Banking Act of 1933, financial institutions were prohibited from simultaneously offering commercial and investment banking services, but with the passage of the Gramm-Leach-Bliley Act of 1999 (GLBA), Congress permitted financial institutions to fully engage in both types of activities.

CHANGES IN FINANCIAL INSTITUTIONS AND THEIR PRODUCTS HAVE SIGNIFICANTLY CHALLENGED THE U.S. FINANCIAL REGULATORY SYSTEM

Several key developments in financial markets and products in the past few decades have significantly challenged the existing financial regulatory structure. (See Figure 1) First, the last 30 years have seen waves of mergers among financial institutions within and across sectors, such that the United States, while still having large numbers of financial institutions, also has several very large globally active financial conglomerates that engage in a wide range of activities that have become increasingly interconnected. Regulators have struggled, and often failed, to mitigate the systemic risks posed by these conglomerates, and to ensure they adequately manage their risks. The portion of firms that conduct activities across the financial sectors of banking, securities, and insurance increased significantly in recent years, but none of the regulators is tasked with assessing the risks posed across the entire financial system.

A second dramatic development in U.S. financial markets in recent decades has been the increasingly critical roles played by less-regulated entities. In the past, consumers of financial products generally dealt with entities such as banks, broker-dealers, and insurance companies that were regulated by a federal or state regulator. However, in the last few decades, various entities—nonbank lenders, hedge funds, credit rating agencies, and special-purpose investment entities—that are not always subject to full regulation by such authorities have become important participants in our financial services markets. These unregulated or less regulated entities can sometimes provide substantial benefits by supplying information or allowing financial institutions to better meet demands of consumers, investors or shareholders, but pose challenges to regulators that do not fully or cannot oversee their activities. For example, significant participation in the subprime mortgage market by generally less-regulated nonbank lenders contributed to a dramatic loosening in underwriting standards leading up to the current financial crisis.

A third development that has revealed limitations in the current regulatory structure has been the proliferation of more complex financial products. In particular, the increasing prevalence of new and more complex investment products has challenged regulators and investors, and consumers have faced difficulty understanding new and increasingly complex retail mortgage and credit products. Regulators failed to adequately oversee the sale of mortgage products that posed risks to consumers and the stability of the financial system.

Developments in financial markets and products		Examples of how developments have challenged the regulatory system
	**Emergence of large, complex, globally active, interconnected financial conglomerates**	Regulators sometimes lack sufficient authority, tools, or capabilities to oversee and mitigate risks
		Identifying, preventing, mitigating, and resolving systemic crises has become more difficult.
	**Less-regulated entities have come to play increasingly critical roles in financial system**	Nonbank lenders and a new private-label securitization market played significant roles in subprime mortgage crisis that led to broader market turmoil
		Activities of hedge funds have posed systemic risks
		Overreliance on credit ratings of mortgage-backed products contributed to the recent turmoil in financial markets
		Financial institutions' use of off-balance sheet entities led to ineffective risk disclosure and exacerbated recent market instability.
	**New and complex products that pose challenges to financial stability and investor and consumer understanding of risks.**	Complex structured finance products have made it difficult for institutions and their regulators to manage associated risks
		Growth in complex and less-regulated over-the-counter derivatives markets have created systemic risks and revealed market infrastructure weaknesses
		Investors have faced difficulty understanding complex investment products, either because they failed to seek out necessary information or were misled by improper sales practices
		Consumers have faced difficulty understanding mortgages and credit cards with new and increasingly complicated features, due in part to limitations in consumer disclosures and financial literacy efforts
		Accounting and auditing entities have faced challenges in trying to ensure that accounting and financial reporting requirements appropriately meet the needs of investors and other financial market participants
	**Financial markets have become increasingly global in nature, and regulators have had to coordinate their efforts internationally.**	Standard setters and regulators also face new challenges in dealing with global convergence of accounting and auditing standards
		Fragmented U.S. regulatory structure has complicated some efforts to coordinate internationally with other regulators, such as negotiations on Basel II and certain insurance matters

Sources: GAO (analysis); Art Explosion (images).

Figure 1. Key Developments and Resulting Challenges That Have Hindered the Effectiveness of the Financial Regulatory System

Fourth, standard setters for accounting and financial regulators have faced growing challenges in ensuring that accounting and audit standards appropriately respond to financial market developments, and in addressing challenges arising from the global convergence of accounting and auditing standards.

Finally, with the increasingly global aspects of financial markets, the current fragmented U.S. regulatory structure has complicated some efforts to coordinate internationally with other regulators. For example, the current system has complicated the ability of financial regulators to convey a single U.S. position in international discussions, such the Basel Accords process for developing international capital standards, and international officials have also indicated that the lack of a single point of contact on, for example, insurance issues has complicated regulatory decision making.

A Framework for Crafting and Assessing Alternatives for Reforming the U.S. Financial Regulatory System

As a result of significant market developments in recent decades that have outpaced a fragmented and outdated regulatory structure, significant reforms to the U.S. regulatory system are critically and urgently needed. The current system has important weaknesses that, if not addressed, will continue to expose the nation's financial system to serious risks. As early as 1994, we identified the need to examine the federal financial regulatory structure, including the need to address the risks from new unregulated products.[3] Since then, we have described various options for Congress to consider, each of which provides potential improvements, as well as some risks and potential costs.[4] Our report offers a framework for crafting and evaluating regulatory reform proposals; it consists of the following nine characteristics that should be reflected in any new regulatory system. By applying the elements of this framework, the relative strengths and weaknesses of any reform proposal should be better revealed, and policymakers should be able to focus on identifying trade-offs and balancing competing goals. Similarly, the framework could be used to craft proposals, or to identify aspects to be added to existing proposals to make them more effective and appropriate for addressing the limitations of the current system.

1. ***Clearly defined regulatory goals.* A regulatory system should have goals that are clearly articulated and relevant, so that regulators can effectively conduct activities to implement their missions.**

A critical first step to modernizing the regulatory system and enhancing its ability to meet the challenges of a dynamic financial services industry is to clearly define regulatory goals and objectives. In the background of our report, we identified four broad goals of financial regulation that regulators have generally sought to achieve. These include ensuring adequate consumer protections, ensuring the integrity and fairness of markets, monitoring the safety and soundness of institutions, and acting to ensure the stability of the overall financial system. However, these goals are not always explicitly set in the federal statutes and regulations that govern these regulators. Having specific goals clearly articulated in legislation could serve to better focus regulators on achieving their missions with greater certainty and purpose, and provide continuity over time.

Given some of the key changes in financial markets discussed in our report—particularly the increased interconnectedness of institutions, the increased complexity of products, and the increasingly global nature of financial markets—Congress should consider the benefits that may result from re-examining the goals of financial regulation and making explicit a set of comprehensive and cohesive goals that reflect today's environment. For example, it may be beneficial to have a clearer focus on ensuring that products are not sold with unsuitable, unfair, deceptive, or abusive features; that systemic risks and the stability of the overall financial system are specifically addressed; or that U.S. firms are competitive in a global environment. This may be especially important given the history of financial regulation and the ad hoc approach through which the existing goals have been established.

We found varying views about the goals of regulation and how they should be prioritized. For example, representatives of some regulatory agencies and industry groups emphasized the importance of creating a competitive financial system, whereas members of one consumer advocacy group noted that reforms should focus on improving regulatory effectiveness rather than addressing concerns about market competitiveness. In addition, as the Federal Reserve notes, financial regulatory goals often will prove interdependent and at other times may conflict.

Revisiting the goals of financial regulation would also help ensure that all involved entities—legislators, regulators, institutions, and consumers—are able to work jointly to meet the intended goals of financial regulation. Such goals and objectives could help establish agency priorities and define responsibility and accountability for identifying risks, including those that cross markets and industries. Policymakers should also carefully define jurisdictional lines and weigh the advantages and disadvantages of having overlapping authorities. While ensuring that the primary goals of financial regulation—including system soundness, market integrity, and consumer protection—are better articulated for regulators, policymakers will also have to ensure that regulation is balanced with other national goals, including facilitating capital raising, innovation, and other benefits that foster long-term growth, stability, and welfare of the United States.

Once these goals are agreed upon, policymakers will need to determine the extent to which goals need to be clarified and specified through rules and requirements, or whether to avoid such specificity and provide regulators with greater flexibility in interpreting such goals. Some reform proposals suggest "principles-based regulation" in which regulators apply broad-based regulatory principles on a case-by-case basis. Such an approach offers the potential advantage of allowing regulators to better adapt to changing market developments. Proponents also note that such an approach would prevent institutions in a more rules-based system from complying with the exact letter of the law while still engaging in unsound or otherwise undesirable financial activities. However, such an approach has potential limitations. Opponents note that regulators may face challenges to implement such a subjective set of principles. A lack of clear rules about activities could lead to litigation if financial institutions and consumers alike disagree with how regulators interpreted goals. Opponents of principles-based regulation note that industry participants who support such an approach have also in many cases advocated for bright-line standards and increased clarity in regulation, which may be counter to a principles-based system. The most effective approach may involve both a set of broad underlying principles and some clear technical rules prohibiting specific activities that have been identified as problematic.

Key issues to be addressed:

- Clarify and update the goals of financial regulation and provide sufficient information on how potentially conflicting goals might be prioritized.
- Determine the appropriate balance of broad principles and specific rules that will result in the most effective and flexible implementation of regulatory goals.

2. ***Appropriately comprehensive.* A regulatory system should ensure that financial institutions and activities are regulated in a way that ensures regulatory goals are fully met. As such, activities that pose risks to consumer protection, financial stability, or other goals should be comprehensively regulated, while recognizing that not all activities will require the same level of regulation.**

A financial regulatory system should effectively meet the goals of financial regulation, as articulated as part of this process, in a way that is appropriately comprehensive. In doing so, policymakers may want to consider how to ensure that both the breadth and depth of regulation are appropriate and adequate. That is, policymakers and regulators should consider how to make determinations about which activities and products, both new and existing, require some aspect of regulatory involvement to meet regulatory goals, and then make determinations about how extensive such regulation should be. As we noted in our report, gaps in the current level of federal oversight of mortgage lenders, credit rating agencies, and certain complex financial products such as CDOs and credit default swaps likely have contributed to the current crisis. Congress and regulators may also want to revisit the extent of regulation for entities such as banks that have traditionally fallen within full federal oversight but for which existing regulatory efforts, such as oversight related to risk management and lending standards, have been proven in some cases inadequate by recent events. However, overly restrictive regulation can stifle the financial sectors' ability to innovate and stimulate capital formation and economic growth. Regulators have struggled to balance these competing objectives, and the current crisis appears to reveal that the proper balance was not in place in the regulatory system to date.

Key issues to be addressed:

- Identify risk-based criteria, such as a product's or institution's potential to harm consumers or create systemic problems, for determining the appropriate level of oversight for financial activities and institutions.
- Identify ways that regulation can provide protection but avoid hampering innovation, capital formation, and economic growth.

3. ***Systemwide focus.* A regulatory system should include a mechanism for identifying, monitoring, and managing risks to the financial system regardless of the source of the risk or the institutions in which it is created.**

A regulatory system should focus on risks to the financial system, not just institutions. As noted in our report, with multiple regulators primarily responsible for individual institutions or markets, none of the financial regulators is tasked with assessing the risks posed across the entire financial system by a few institutions or by the collective activities of the industry. The collective activities of a number of entities—including mortgage brokers, real estate professionals, lenders, borrowers, securities underwriters, investors, rating agencies and others—likely all contributed to the recent market crisis, but no one regulator had the necessary scope of oversight to identify the risks to the broader financial system. Similarly, once firms began to fail and the full extent of the financial crisis began to become clear, no formal mechanism existed to monitor market trends and potentially stop or help mitigate the fallout from these events.

Having a single entity responsible for assessing threats to the overall financial system could prevent some of the crises that we have seen in the past. For example, in its *Blueprint for a Modernized Financial Regulatory Structure*, Treasury proposed expanding the responsibilities of the Federal Reserve to create a "market stability regulator" that would have broad authority to gather and disclose appropriate information, collaborate with other regulators on rulemaking, and take corrective action as necessary in the interest of overall financial market stability. Such a regulator could assess the systemic risks that arise at financial institutions, within specific financial sectors, across the nation, and globally. However, policymakers should consider that a potential disadvantage of providing the agency with such broad responsibility for overseeing nonbank entities could be that it may imply an official government support or endorsement, such as a government guarantee, of such activities, and thus encourage greater risk taking by these financial institutions and investors.

Regardless of whether a new regulator is created, all regulators under a new system should consider how their activities could better identify and address systemic risks posed by their institutions. As the Federal Reserve Chairman has noted, regulation and supervision of financial institutions is a critical tool for limiting systemic risk. This will require broadening the focus from individual safety and soundness of institutions to a systemwide oversight approach that includes potential systemic risks and weaknesses.

A systemwide focus should also increase attention on how the incentives and constraints created by regulations affects risk taking throughout the business cycle, and what actions regulators can take to anticipate and mitigate such risks. However, as the Federal Reserve Chairman has noted, the more comprehensive the approach, the more technically demanding and costly it would be for regulators and affected institutions.

Key issues to be addressed:

- Identify approaches to broaden the focus of individual regulators or establish new regulatory mechanisms for identifying and acting on systemic risks.
- Determine what additional authorities a regulator or regulators should have to monitor and act to reduce systemic risks.

4. ***Flexible and adaptable.* A regulatory system should be adaptable and forward-looking such that regulators can readily adapt to market innovations and changes and include a mechanism for evaluating potential new risks to the system.**

A regulatory system should be designed such that regulators can readily adapt to market innovations and changes and include a formal mechanism for evaluating the full potential range of risks of new products and services to the system, market participants, and customers. An effective system could include a mechanism for monitoring market developments— such as broad market changes that introduce systemic risk, or new products and services that may pose more confined risks to particular market segments—to determine the degree, if any, to which regulatory intervention might be required.

The rise of a very large market for credit derivatives, while providing benefits to users, also created exposures that warranted actions by regulators to rescue large individual participants in this market. While efforts are under way to create risk-reducing clearing mechanisms for this market, a more adaptable and responsive regulatory system might have recognized this need earlier and addressed it sooner. Some industry representatives have suggested that principles-based regulation would provide such a mechanism. Designing a system to be flexible and proactive also involves determining whether Congress, regulators, or both should make such determinations, and how such an approach should be clarified in laws or regulations.

Important questions also exist about the extent to which financial regulators should actively monitor and, where necessary, approve new financial products and services as they are developed to ensure the least harm from inappropriate products. Some individuals commenting on this framework, including industry representatives, noted that limiting government intervention in new financial activities until it has become clear that a particular activity or market poses a significant risk and therefore warrants intervention may be more appropriate.

As with other key policy questions, this may be answered with a combination of both approaches, recognizing that a product approval approach may be appropriate for some innovations with greater potential risk, while other activities may warrant a more reactive approach.

Key issues to be addressed:

- Determine how to effectively monitor market developments to identify potential risks; the degree, if any, to which regulatory intervention might be required; and who should hold such a responsibility.
- Consider how to strike the right balance between overseeing new products as they come onto the market to take action as needed to protect consumers and investors, without unnecessarily hindering innovation.

5. ***Efficient and effective.* A regulatory system should provide efficient oversight of financial services by eliminating overlapping federal regulatory missions, where appropriate, and minimizing regulatory burden while effectively achieving the goals of regulation.**

A regulatory system should provide for the efficient and effective oversight of financial services. Accomplishing this in a regulatory system involves many considerations. First, an efficient regulatory system is designed to accomplish its regulatory goals using the least amount of public resources. In this sense, policymakers must consider the number, organization, and responsibilities of each agency, and eliminate undesirable overlap in agency activities and responsibilities. Determining what is undesirable overlap is a difficult decision in itself. Under the current U.S. system, financial institutions often have several options for how to operate their business and who will be their regulator. For example, a new or existing depository institution can choose among several charter options. Having multiple regulators performing similar functions does allow for these agencies to potentially develop alternative or innovative approaches to regulation separately, with the approach working best becoming known over time. Such proven approaches can then be adopted by the other agencies. On the other hand, this could lead to regulatory arbitrage, in which institutions take advantage of variations in how agencies implement regulatory responsibilities in order to be subject to less scrutiny. Both situations have occurred under our current structure.

With that said, recent events clearly have shown that the fragmented U.S. regulatory structure contributed to failures by the existing regulators to adequately protect consumers and ensure financial stability. As we note in our report, efforts by regulators to respond to the increased risks associated with new mortgage products were sometimes slowed in part because of the need for five federal regulators to coordinate their response. The Chairman of the Federal Reserve has similarly noted that the different regulatory and supervisory regimes for lending institutions and mortgage brokers made monitoring such institutions difficult for both regulators and investors. Similarly, we noted in our report that the current fragmented U.S. regulatory structure has complicated some efforts to coordinate internationally with other regulators.

One first step to addressing such problems is to seriously consider the need to consolidate depository institution oversight among fewer agencies. Since 1996, we have been recommending that the number of federal agencies with primary responsibilities for bank oversight be reduced.[5] Such a move would result in a system that was more efficient and improve consistency in regulation, another important characteristic of an effective regulatory system. In addition, Congress could consider the advantages and disadvantages of providing a federal charter option for insurance and creating a federal insurance regulatory entity. We have not studied the issue of an optional federal charter for insurers, but have through the years noted difficulties with efforts to harmonize insurance regulation across states through the NAIC-based structure. The establishment of a federal insurance charter and regulator could help alleviate some of these challenges, but such an approach could also have unintended consequences for state regulatory bodies and for insurance firms as well.

Also, given the challenges associated with increasingly complex investment and retail products as discussed earlier, policymakers will need to consider how best to align agency responsibilities to better ensure that consumers and investors are provided with clear, concise, and effective disclosures for all products.

Organizing agencies around regulatory goals as opposed to the existing sector-based regulation may be one way to improve the effectiveness of the system, especially given some of the market developments discussed earlier. Whatever the approach, policymakers should seek to minimize conflict in regulatory goals across regulators, or provide for efficient mechanisms to coordinate in cases where goals inevitably overlap. For example, in some cases, the safety and soundness of an individual institution may have implications for systemic risk, or addressing an unfair or deceptive act or practice at a financial institution may have implications on the institution's safety and soundness by increasing reputational risk. If a regulatory system assigns these goals to different regulators, it will be important to establish mechanisms for them to coordinate.

Proposals to consolidate regulatory agencies for the purpose of promoting efficiency should also take into account any potential trade-offs related to effectiveness. For example, to the extent that policymakers see value in the ability of financial institutions to choose their regulator, consolidating certain agencies may reduce such benefits. Similarly, some individuals have commented that the current system of multiple regulators has led to the development of expertise among agency staff in particular areas of financial market activities that might be threatened if the system were to be consolidated. Finally, policymakers may want to ensure that any transition from the current financial system to a new structure should minimize as best as possible any disruption to the operation of financial markets or risks to the government, especially given the current challenges faced in today's markets and broader economy.

A financial system should also be efficient by minimizing the burden on regulated entities to the extent possible while still achieving regulatory goals. Under our current system, many financial institutions, and especially large institutions that offer services that cross sectors, are subject to supervision by multiple regulators. While steps toward consolidated supervision and designating primary supervisors have helped alleviate some of the burden, industry representatives note that many institutions face significant costs as a result of the existing financial regulatory system that could be lessened. Such costs, imposed in an effort to meet certain regulatory goals such as safety and soundness and consumer protection, can run counter to other goals of a financial system by stifling innovation and competitiveness. In addressing this concern, it is also important to consider the potential benefits that might result in some cases from having multiple regulators overseeing an institution. For example, representatives of state banking and other institution regulators, and consumer advocacy organizations, note that concurrent jurisdiction— between two federal regulators or a federal and state regulator—can provide needed checks and balances against individual financial regulators who have not always reacted appropriately and in a timely way to address problems at institutions. They also note that states may move more quickly and more flexibly to respond to activities causing harm to consumers. Some types of concurrent jurisdiction, such as enforcement authority, may be less burdensome to institutions than others, such as ongoing supervision and examination.

Key issues to be addressed:

- Consider the appropriate role of the states in a financial regulatory system and how federal and state roles can be better harmonized.
- Determine and evaluate the advantages and disadvantages of having multiple regulators, including nongovernmental entities such as SROs, share responsibilities for regulatory oversight.
- Identify ways that the U.S. regulatory system can be made more efficient, either through consolidating agencies with similar roles or through minimizing unnecessary regulatory burden.
- Consider carefully how any changes to the financial regulatory system may negatively impact financial market operations and the broader economy, and take steps to minimize such consequences.

6. ***Consistent consumer and investor protection.* A regulatory system should include consumer and investor protection as part of the regulatory mission to ensure that market participants receive consistent, useful information, as well as legal protections for similar financial products and services, including disclosures, sales practice standards, and suitability requirements.**

A regulatory system should be designed to provide high-quality, effective, and consistent protection for consumers and investors in similar situations. In doing so, it is important to recognize important distinctions between retail consumers and more sophisticated consumers such as institutional investors, where appropriate considering the context of the situation. Different disclosures and regulatory protections may be necessary for these different groups. Consumer protection should be viewed from the perspective of the consumer rather than through the various and sometimes divergent perspectives of the multitude of federal regulators that currently have responsibilities in this area.

As discussed in our report, many consumers that received loans in the last few years did not understand the risks associated with taking out their loans, especially in the event that housing prices would not continue to increase at the rate they had in recent years. In addition, increasing evidence exists that many Americans are lacking in financial literacy, and the expansion of new and more complex products will continue to create challenges in this area. Furthermore, regulators with existing authority to better protect consumers did not always exercise that authority effectively. In considering a new regulatory system, policymakers should consider the significant lapses in our regulatory system's focus on consumer protection and ensure that such a focus is prioritized in any reform efforts. For example, policymakers should identify ways to improve upon the existing, largely fragmented, system of regulators that must coordinate to act in these areas. This should include serious consideration of whether to consolidate regulatory responsibilities to streamline and improve the effectiveness of consumer protection efforts. Another way that some market observers have argued that consumer protections could be enhanced and harmonized across products is to extend suitability requirements—which require securities brokers making recommendations to customers to have reasonable grounds for believing that the recommendation is suitable for the customer—to mortgage and other products. Additional consideration could also be given to determining whether certain products are simply too complex to be well understood and make judgments about limiting or curtailing their use.

Key issues to be addressed:

- Consider how prominent the regulatory goal of consumer protection should be in the U.S. financial regulatory system.
- Determine what amount, if any, of consolidation of responsibility may be necessary to enhance and harmonize consumer protections, including suitability requirements and disclosures across the financial services industry.
- Consider what distinctions are necessary between retail and wholesale products, and how such distinctions should affect how they are regulated.

- Identify opportunities to protect and empower consumers through improving their financial literacy.

7. ***Regulators provided with independence, prominence, authority, and accountability*. A regulatory system should ensure that regulators have independence from inappropriate influence; have sufficient resources, clout, and authority to carry out and enforce statutory missions; and are clearly accountable for meeting regulatory goals.**

A regulatory system should ensure that any entity responsible for financial regulation is independent from inappropriate influence; has adequate prominence, authority, and resources to carry out and enforce its statutory mission; and is clearly accountable for meeting regulatory goals. With respect to independence, policymakers may want to consider advantages and disadvantages of different approaches to funding agencies, especially to the extent that agencies might face difficulty remaining independent if they are funded by the institutions they regulate. Under the current structure, for example, the Federal Reserve primarily is funded by income earned from U.S. government securities that it has acquired through open market operations and does not assess charges to the institutions it oversees. In contrast, OCC and OTS are funded primarily by assessments on the firms they supervise. Decision makers should consider whether some of these various funding mechanisms are more likely to ensure that a regulator will take action against its regulated institutions without regard to the potential impact on its own funding.

With respect to prominence, each regulator must receive appropriate attention and support from top government officials. Inadequate prominence in government may make it difficult for a regulator to raise safety and soundness or other concerns to Congress and the administration in a timely manner. Mere knowledge of a deteriorating situation would be insufficient if a regulator were unable to persuade Congress and the administration to take timely corrective action. This problem would be exacerbated if a regulated institution had more political clout and prominence than its regulator because the institution could potentially block action from being taken.

In considering authority, agencies must have the necessary enforcement and other tools to effectively implement their missions to achieve regulatory goals. For example, in a 2007 report we expressed concerns over the appropriateness of having OTS oversee diverse global financial firms given the size of the agency relative to the institutions for which it was responsible.[6] It is important for a regulatory system to ensure that agencies are provided with adequate resources and expertise to conduct their work effectively. A regulatory system should also include adequate checks and balances to ensure the appropriate use of agency authorities. With respect to accountability, policymakers may also want to consider different governance structures at agencies—the current system includes a combination of agency heads and independent boards or commissions— and how to ensure that agencies are recognized for successes and held accountable for failures to act in accordance with regulatory goals.

Key issues to be addressed:

- Determine how to structure and fund agencies to ensure each has adequate independence, prominence, tools, authority and accountability.
- Consider how to provide an appropriate level of authority to an agency while ensuring that it appropriately implements its mission without abusing its authority.
- Ensure that the regulatory system includes effective mechanisms for holding regulators accountable.

8. *Consistent financial oversight.* A regulatory system should ensure that similar institutions, products, risks, and services are subject to consistent regulation, oversight, and transparency, which should help minimize negative competitive outcomes while harmonizing oversight, both within the United States and internationally.

A regulatory system should ensure that similar institutions, products, and services posing similar risks are subject to consistent regulation, oversight, and transparency. Identifying which institutions and which of their products and services pose similar risks is not easy and involves a number of important considerations. Two institutions that look very similar may in fact pose very different risks to the financial system, and therefore may call for significantly different regulatory treatment.

However, activities that are done by different types of financial institutions that pose similar risks to their institutions or the financial system should be regulated similarly to prevent competitive disadvantages between institutions.

Streamlining the regulation of similar products across sectors could also help prepare the United States for challenges that may result from increased globalization and potential harmonization in regulatory standards. Such efforts are under way in other jurisdictions. For example, at a November 2008 summit in the United States, the Group of 20 countries pledged to strengthen their regulatory regimes and ensure that all financial markets, products, and participants are consistently regulated or subject to oversight, as appropriate to their circumstances. Similarly, a working group in the European Union is slated by the spring of 2009 to propose ways to strengthen European supervisory arrangements, including addressing how their supervisors should cooperate with other major jurisdictions to help safeguard financial stability globally. Promoting consistency in regulation of similar products should be done in a way that does not sacrifice the quality of regulatory oversight.

As we noted in a 2004 report, different regulatory treatment of bank and financial holding companies, consolidated supervised entities, and other holding companies may not provide a basis for consistent oversight of their consolidated risk management strategies, guarantee competitive neutrality, or contribute to better oversight of systemic risk.[7] Recent events further underscore the limitations brought about when there is a lack of consistency in oversight of large financial institutions. As such, Congress and regulators will need to seriously consider how best to consolidate responsibilities for oversight of large financial conglomerates as part of any reform effort.

Key issues to be addressed:

- Identify institutions and products and services that pose similar risks.
- Determine the level of consolidation necessary to streamline financial regulation activities across the financial services industry.
- Consider the extent to which activities need to be coordinated internationally.

9. ***Minimal taxpayer exposure.* A regulatory system should have adequate safeguards that allow financial institution failures to occur while limiting taxpayers' exposure to financial risk.**

A regulatory system should have adequate safeguards that allow financial institution failures to occur while limiting taxpayers' exposure to financial risk. Policymakers should consider identifying the best safeguards and assignment of responsibilities for responding to situations where taxpayers face significant exposures, and should consider providing clear guidelines when regulatory intervention is appropriate. While an ideal system would allow firms to fail without negatively affecting other firms— and therefore avoid any moral hazard that may result—policymakers and regulators must consider the realities of today's financial system. In some cases, the immediate use of public funds to prevent the failure of a critically important financial institution may be a worthwhile use of such funds if it ultimately serves to prevent a systemic crisis that would result in much greater use of public funds in the long run. However, an effective regulatory system that incorporates the characteristics noted previously, especially by ensuring a systemwide focus, should be better equipped to identify and mitigate problems before it become necessary to make decisions about whether to let a financial institution fail.

An effective financial regulatory system should also strive to minimize systemic risks resulting from interrelationships between firms and limitations in market infrastructures that prevent the orderly unwinding of firms that fail. Another important consideration in minimizing taxpayer exposure is to ensure that financial institutions provided with a government guarantee that could result in taxpayer exposure are also subject to an appropriate level of regulatory oversight to fulfill their responsibilities.

Key issues to be addressed:

- Identify safeguards that are most appropriate to prevent systemic crises while minimizing moral hazard.
- Consider how a financial system can most effectively minimize taxpayer exposure to losses related to financial instability.

Finally, although significant changes may be required to modernize the U.S. financial regulatory system, policymakers should consider carefully how best to implement the changes in such a way that the transition to a new structure does not hamper the functioning of the financial markets, individual financial institutions' ability to conduct their activities, and consumers' ability to access needed services. For example, if the changes require regulators or institutions to make systems changes, file registrations, or other activities that could require extensive time to complete, the changes could be implemented in phases with specific target dates around which the affected entities could formulate plans. In addition, our past work has identified certain critical factors that should be addressed to ensure that any large-scale transitions among government agencies are implemented successfully.[8] Although all of these factors are likely important for a successful transformation for the financial regulatory system, Congress and existing agencies should pay particular attention to ensuring there are effective communication strategies so that all affected parties, including investors and consumers, clearly understand any changes being implemented. In addition, attention should be paid to developing a sound human capital strategy to ensure that any new or consolidated agencies are able to retain and attract additional quality staff during the transition period. Finally, policymakers should consider how best to retain and utilize the existing skills and knowledge base within agencies subject to changes as part of a transition.

Mr. Chairman and Members of the Committee, I appreciate the opportunity to discuss these critically important issues and would be happy to answer any questions that you may have. Thank you.

End Notes

[1] GAO, *Financial Regulation: A Framework for Crafting and Assessing Proposals to Modernize the Outdated U.S. Financial Regulatory System*, GAO-09-216 (Washington, D.C.: Jan. 8, 2009).

[2] GAO, *High Risk Series: An Update*, GAO-09-271 (Washington, D.C.: Jan. 22, 2009).

[3] GAO, *Financial Derivatives: Actions Needed to Protect the Financial System*, GAO/GGD-94-133 (Washington, D.C.: May 18, 1994).

[4] GAO, *Financial Regulation: Industry Changes Prompt Need to Reconsider U.S. Regulatory Structure*, GAO-05-61 (Washington, D.C.: Oct. 6, 2004); and *Financial Regulation: Industry Trends Continue to Challenge the Federal Regulatory Structure*, GAO-08-32 (Washington, D.C.: Oct. 12, 2007).

[5] See GAO, *Bank Oversight: Fundamental Principles for Modernizing the U.S. Structure*, GAO/T-GGD-96-117 (Washington, D.C.: May 2, 1996).

[6] GAO, *Financial Market Regulation: Agencies Engaged in Consolidated Supervision Can Strengthen Performance Measurement and Collaboration*, GAO-07-154 (Washington, D.C.: Mar. 15, 2007).

[7] GAO-05-61.

[8] See GAO, Homeland Security: Critical Design and Implementation Issues, GAO-02-957T (Washington, D.C.: July 17, 2002).

In: Financial Regulatory Reform
Editors: Stephen E. Moyer

ISBN: 978-1-60741-567-1

Chapter 2

SPECIAL REPORT ON REGULATORY REFORM: MODERNIZING THE AMERICAN FINANCIAL REGULATORY SYSTEM: RECOMMENDATIONS FOR IMPROVING OVER-SIGHT, PROTECTING CONSUMERS AND ENSURING STABILITY*

Congressional Oversight Panel

I. EXECUTIVE SUMMARY

1. Lessons from the Past

Financial crises are not new. As early as 1792, during the presidency of George Washington, the nation suffered a severe panic that froze credit and nearly brought the young economy to its knees. Over the next 140 years, financial crises struck on a regular basis—in 1797, 1819, 1837, 1857, 1873, 1893–96, 1907, and 1929–33—roughly every fifteen to twenty years.

But as the United States emerged from the Great Depression, something remarkable happened: the crises stopped. New financial regulation—including federal deposit insurance, securities regulation, and banking supervision—effectively protected the system from devastating outbreaks. Economic growth returned, but recurrent financial crises did not. In time, a financial crisis was seen as a ghost of the past.

After fifty years without a financial crisis—the longest such stretch in the nation's history— financial firms and policy makers began to see regulation as a barrier to efficient functioning of the capital markets rather than a necessary precondition for success.

This change in attitude had unfortunate consequences. As financial markets grew and globalized, often with breathtaking speed, the U.S. regulatory system could have benefited from smart changes. But deregulation and the growth of unregulated, parallel shadow markets were accompanied by the nearly unrestricted marketing of increasingly complex consumer financial products that multiplied risk at every stratum of the economy, from the family level to the global level. The result proved disastrous. The first warning followed deregulation of the thrifts, when the country suffered the savings and loan crisis in the 1980s. A second warning came in 1998 when a crisis was only narrowly averted following the failure of a large unregulated hedge fund. The near financial panic of 2002, brought on by corporate accounting and governance failures, sounded a third warning.

The United States now faces its worst financial crisis since the Great Depression. It is critical that the lessons of that crisis be studied to restore a proper balance between free markets and the regulatory framework necessary to ensure the operation of those markets to protect the economy, honest market participants, and the public.

2. Shortcomings of the Present

The current crisis should come as no surprise. The present regulatory system has failed to effectively manage risk, require sufficient transparency, and ensure fair dealings.

Financial markets are inherently volatile and prone to extremes. The government has a critical role to play in helping to manage both public and private risk. Without clear and effective rules in place, productive financial activity can degenerate into unproductive gambling, while sophisticated financial transactions, as well as more ordinary consumer credit transactions, can give way to swindles and fraud.

A well-regulated financial system serves a key public purpose: if it has the power and if its leaders have the will to use that power, it channels savings and investment into productive economic activity and helps prevent financial contagion. Like the management of any complex hazard, financial regulation should not rely on a single magic bullet, but instead should employ an array of related measures for managing various elements of risk. The advent of the automobile brought enormous benefits but also considerable risks to drivers, passengers, and pedestrians. The solution was not to prohibit driving, but rather to manage the risks through reasonable speed limits, better road construction, safer sidewalks, required safety devices (seatbelts, airbags, children's car seats, antilock breaks), mandatory automobile insurance, and so on. The same holds true in the financial sector.

In recent years, however, the regulatory system not only failed to manage risk, it also failed to require disclosure of risk through sufficient transparency. American financial markets are profoundly dependent upon transparency. After all, the fundamental risk/reward corollary depends on the ability of market participants to have confidence in their ability to accurately judge risk.

Markets have become opaque in multiple ways. Some markets, such as hedge funds and credit default swaps, provide virtually no information. Even so, disclosure alone does not always provide genuine transparency. Market participants must have useful, relevant information delivered in an appropriate, timely manner. Recent market occurrences involving off-balance-sheet entities and complex financial instruments reveal the lack of transparency resulting from the wrong information disclosed at the wrong time and in the wrong manner. Mortgage documentation suffers from a similar problem, with reams of paper thrust at borrowers at closing, far too late for any borrower to make a well-informed decision. Just as markets and financial products evolve, so too must efforts to provide understanding through genuine transparency.

To compound the problem associated with uncontained and opaque risks, the current regulatory framework has failed to ensure fair dealings. Unfair dealing can be blatant, such as outright deception or fraud, but unfairness can also be much more subtle, as when parties are unfairly matched. Individuals have limited time and expertise to master complex financial dealings. If one party to a transaction has significantly more resources, time, sophistication or experience, other parties are at a fundamental disadvantage. The regulatory system should take appropriate steps to level the playing field.

Unfair dealings affect not only the specific transaction participants, but extend across entire markets, neighborhoods, socioeconomic groups, and whole industries. Even when only a limited number of families in one neighborhood have been the direct victims of a predatory lender, the entire neighborhood and even the larger community will suffer very real consequences from the resulting foreclosures. As those consequences spread, the entire financial system can be affected as well. More importantly, unfairness, or even the perception of unfairness, causes a loss of confidence in the marketplace. It becomes all the more critical for regulators to ensure fairness through meaningful disclosure, consumer protection measures, stronger enforcement, and other measures. Fair dealings provide credibility to businesses and satisfaction to consumers.

In tailoring regulatory responses to these and other problems, the goal should always be to strike a reasonable balance between the costs of regulation and its benefits. Just as speed limits are more stringent on busy city streets than on open highways, financial regulation should be strictest where the threats—especially the threats to other citizens—are greatest, and it should be more moderate elsewhere.

3. Recommendations for the Future

Modern financial regulation can provide consumers and investors with adequate information for making sound financial decisions and can protect them from being misled or defrauded, especially in complex financial transactions. Better regulation can reduce conflicts of interest and help manage moral hazard, particularly by limiting incentives for excessive risk taking stemming from often implicit government guaranties. By limiting risk taking in key parts of the financial sector, regulation can reduce systemic threats to the broader financial system and the economy as a whole. Ultimately, financial regulation embodies good risk management, transparency, and fairness.

Had regulators given adequate attention to even one of the three key areas of risk management, transparency and fairness, we might have averted the worst aspects of the current crisis.

1. Risk management should have been addressed through better oversight of systemic risks. If companies that are now deemed "too big to fail" had been better regulated, either to diminish their systemic impact or to curtail the risks they took, then these companies could have been allowed to fail or to reorganize without taxpayer bailouts. The creation of any new implicit government guarantee of high-risk business activities could have been avoided.
2. Transparency should have been addressed though better, more accurate credit ratings. If companies issuing high-risk credit instruments had not been able to obtain AAA ratings from the private

credit rating agencies, then pension funds, financial institutions, state and local municipalities, and others that relied on those ratings would not have been misled into making dangerous investments.

3. Fairness should have been addressed though better regulation of consumer financial products. If the excesses in mortgage lending had been curbed by even the most minimal consumer protection laws, the loans that were fed into the mortgage backed securities would have been choked off at the source, and there would have been no "toxic assets" to threaten the global economy.

While the current crisis had many causes, it was not unforeseeable. Correcting the mistakes that fueled this crisis is within reach. The challenge now is to develop a new set of rules for a new financial system.

The Panel has identified eight specific areas most urgently in need of reform:

1. Identify and regulate financial institutions that pose systemic risk.
2. Limit excessive leverage in American financial institutions.
3. Increase supervision of the shadow financial system.
4. Create a new system for federal and state regulation of mortgages and other consumer credit products.
5. Create executive pay structures that discourage excessive risk taking.
6. Reform the credit rating system.
7. Make establishing a global financial regulatory floor a U.S. diplomatic priority.
8. Plan for the next crisis.

While these are the most pressing reform recommendations, many other issues merit further study, the results of which the Panel will present in future reports. Despite the magnitude of the task, the central message is clear: through modernized regulation, we can dramatically reduce the risk of crises and swindles while preserving the key benefits of a vibrant financial system

Americans have paid dearly for this latest crisis. Lost jobs, failed businesses, foreclosed homes, and sharply cut retirement savings have touched people all across the county. Now every citizen—even the most prudent—is called on to assume trillions of dollars in liabilities spent to try to repair a broken system. The costs of regulatory failure and the urgency of regulatory reform could not be clearer.

II. Introduction

The financial crisis that began to take hold in 2007 has exposed significant weaknesses in the nation's financial architecture and in the regulatory system designed to ensure its safety, stability, and performance. In fact, there can be no avoiding the conclusion that our regulatory system has failed.

The bursting of the housing bubble produced the first true stress test of modern capital markets, their instruments, and their participants. The first cracks were evident in the subprime mortgage market and in the secondary market for mortgage-related securities. From there, the crisis spread to nearly every corner of the financial sector, both at home and abroad, taking down some of the most venerable names in the investment banking and insurance businesses and crippling others, wreaking havoc in the credit markets, and brutalizing equity markets worldwide.

As asset prices deflated, so too did the theory that had increasingly guided American financial regulation over the previous three decades—namely, that private markets and private financial institutions could largely be trusted to regulate themselves. The crisis suggested otherwise, particularly since several of the least regulated parts of the system were among the first to run into trouble. As former Federal Reserve Chairman Alan Greenspan acknowledged in testimony before the House Committee on Oversight and Government Reform in October 2008, "Those of us who have looked to the self-interest of lending institutions to protect shareholders' equity, myself included, are in a state of shocked disbelief."[1]

The financial meltdown necessitates a thorough review of our regulatory infrastructure, the behavior of regulators and their agencies, and the regulatory philosophy that informed their decisions. At the same time, we must be careful to avoid the trap of looking solely backward—preparing to fight the last war. Although the crisis has exposed many deficiencies, there are likely others that have yet to be uncovered. What is more, the vast federal response to the crisis—including unprecedented rescues of crippled businesses and a proliferation of government guaranties—threatens to distort private incentives in the future, further eroding the caution of financial creditors and making the job of regulatory oversight all the more essential.

Realizing that far-reaching reform will be needed in the wake of the crisis, Congress directed the Congressional Oversight Panel (hereinafter "the Panel") to submit a special report on regulatory reform,

> analyzing the current state of the regulatory system and its effectiveness at overseeing the participants in the financial system and protecting consumers, and providing recommendations for improvement, including recommendations regarding whether any participants in the financial markets that are currently outside the regulatory system should become subject to the regulatory system, the rationale underlying such recommendation, and whether there are any gaps in existing consumer protections.[2]

Toward this end, part III of this report presents a broad framework for analyzing the effectiveness of financial regulation, focusing on three critical failures of the current system: (1) inadequate private and public risk management, (2) insufficient transparency and information, and (3) a lack of protection against deception and unfair dealing. These key failures of the regulatory system have manifested themselves in a plethora of more specific problems, ranging from excessively leveraged financial institutions to opaque financial instruments falling outside the scope of the jurisdiction of any regulatory agency. While this report cannot tackle every one of these problems, part IV focuses on eight areas of the current financial regulatory system that are in need of improvement, offering the Panel's recommendations for each as follows:

1. Identify and regulate financial institutions that pose systemic risk.
2. Limit excessive leverage in American financial institutions.
3. Modernize supervision of the shadow financial system.
4. Create a new system for federal and state regulation of mortgages and other consumer credit products.
5. Create executive pay structures that discourage excessive risk taking.
6. Reform the credit rating system.
7. Make establishing a global financial regulatory floor a U.S. diplomatic priority.
8. Plan for the next crisis.

Finally, part V of this report points to some additional challenges in need of attention over the longer term, several of which will be addressed in future reports of the Panel. An appendix comprising summaries of other recent reports regarding reform of the regulatory system is found at the end of the report.

This report is motivated by the knowledge that millions of Americans suffer when the financial regulatory system and the capital markets fail. The financial meltdown has many causes but one overwhelming result: a great increase in unexpected hardships and financial challenges for American citizens. The unemployment rate is rising sharply every month, a growing number of Americans are facing the prospect of losing their homes, retirees are worried about how to afford even basic necessities, and families are anxious about paying for college and securing a decent start in adult life. The goal of the regulatory reforms presented in this report is not to endorse a particular economic theory or merely to guide the country through the current crisis. The goal is instead to establish a sturdy regulatory system that will facilitate the growth of financial markets and will protect the lives of current and future generations of Americans.

III. A FRAMEWORK FOR ANALYZING THE FINANCIAL REGULATORY SYSTEM AND ITS EFFECTIVENESS

1. The Promise and Perils of Financial Markets

Households, firms, and government agencies all rely on the financial system for saving and raising capital, settling payments, and managing risk. A dynamic financial system facilitates the mobilization of resources for large projects and the transfer of resources across time and space and provides critical information in the form of price signals that help to coordinate dispersed economic activity. A healthy financial system, one that allows for the efficient allocation of capital and risk, is indispensable to any successful economy.

Unfortunately, financial systems are also prone to instability and abuse. Until the dawn of modern financial regulation in the 1930s and early 1940s, financial panics were a regular—and often debilitating—feature of American life. The United States suffered significant financial crises in 1792, 1819, 1837–39, 1857, 1873, 1893–95, 1907, and 1929–33. After the Great Depression and the introduction of federal deposit insurance and federal banking and securities regulation, the next significant banking crisis did not strike for more than forty years. This period of relative stability—by far the longest in the nation's history—persisted until the mid-1980s, with the onset of the savings and loan crisis; dealing with that crisis cost American taxpayers directly some $132 billion.[3] The country also suffered a group of bank failures that produced the need to recapitalize the FDIC's initial Bank Insurance Fund in the early 1990s; suffered a stock market crash in 1987; witnessed a wave of foreign currency crises (and associated instability) in 1994–95 and 1997–98; saw the collapse of Long Term Capital Management (LCTM) hedge fund in 1998; and faced the collapse of the tech bubble in 2001. Financial crisis has now struck again, with the subprime-induced financial turmoil of 2007–09.

Although every crisis is distinctive in its particulars, the commonalities across crises are often more striking than the differences. As the financial historian Robert Wright explains: "All major panics follow the same basic outline: asset bubble, massive leverage (borrowing to buy the rising asset), bursting bubble (asset price declines rapidly), defaults on loans, asymmetric information and uncertainty, reduced lending, declining economic activity, unemployment, more defaults."[4]

Nor are financial panics the only cause for concern. Financial markets have also long exhibited a vulnerability to manipulation, swindles, and fraud, including William Duer's notorious attempt to corner the market for United States government bonds in 1791–92, the "wildcat" life insurance companies of the early nineteenth century (which took premiums from customers but disappeared before paying any claims), the infamous pyramiding scheme of Charles Ponzi in 1920, and the highly suspect practices of New York's National City Bank and its chairman, Charles Mitchell, in the run-up to the Great Crash of 1929. The apparent massive Ponzi scheme of Bernard Madoff that has recently unraveled in 2008 is only the latest in a long series of such financial scandals.

Even apart from the most spectacular financial crises and crimes, the failure of any individual financial institution—all by itself—can have devastating consequences for the investors and clients who rely on it.[5] The collapse of a bank, insurance company, or pension fund can prove particularly damaging, disrupting longstanding financial relationships and potentially destroying the safety nets that many Americans have spent years carefully building.

The good news is that many of these financial risks can be significantly attenuated through sound regulation. Well-designed regulation has the potential to enhance both financial safety and economic performance, and it has done so in the past. To be sure, the risks of capital market crises cannot be eliminated altogether, just as the risk of automobile accidents will never entirely disappear, despite rigorous safety standards.

2. The Current State of the Regulatory System

The purpose of financial regulation is to make financial markets work better and to ensure that they serve the interests of all Americans. There are many important (and sometimes competing) goals of financial regulation, ranging from safety and stability to innovation and growth. In order to achieve these goals, an effective regulatory system must manage risk, facilitate transparency, and promote fair dealings among market actors. The current system has failed on all three counts.

Failure to Effectively Manage Risk

As the current financial meltdown makes clear, private financial markets do not always manage risk effectively on their own. In fact, to a large extent, the current crisis can be understood as the product of a profound failure in private risk management, combined with an equally profound failure in public risk management, particularly at the federal level.

Failure of private risk management

The risk-management lapses in the private sector are by now obvious. In the subprime market, brokers and originators often devoted relatively little attention to risk assessment, exhibiting a willingness to issue extraordinarily risky mortgages (for high fees) so long as the mortgages could be sold quickly on the secondary market.[6] Securitizers on Wall Street and elsewhere proved hungry for these high-interest-rate loans, because they could earn large fees for bundling them, dividing the payments into tranches, and selling the resulting securities to investors. These securities proved attractive, even to relatively risk-averse investors, because the credit rating agencies (who were paid by the issuers) awarded their triple-A seal of approval to the vast majority of the securities in any given issue. The credit rating agencies concluded—wrongly, it turns out—that virtually all of the risk of a subprime mortgage-backed securitization was concentrated in its lowest tranches (e.g., the bottom 15 to 25 percent) and that the remainder was exceedingly safe. Nor did the process end there, since lower-tranche securities (e.g., those with a BBB rating or below) could be aggregated into so-called collateralized debt obligations (CDOs) and re-tranched, creating whole new sets of AAA and AA securities. Only when the housing market turned down and delinquencies and foreclosures started to rise, beginning in 2006–07, did the issuers, investors, and rating agencies finally recognize how severely they had underestimated the key risks involved.[7]

Had these excesses been limited to the subprime market, it is unlikely that the initial turmoil could have sparked a full-blown financial crisis. Unfortunately, the broader financial system was in no position to absorb the losses because a great many of the leading financial firms were themselves heavily leveraged (especially by incurring a large proportion of short-term debt) and contingent liabilities (including many tied back to the housing market). Such leverage had greatly magnified returns in good times, but proved devastating once key assets began to drop in value. Higher-leverage necessarily meant higher risk. As it became clear that not only AAA-rated mortgage- backed securities but also AAA-rated financial institutions were at risk, trust all but disappeared in the marketplace, leaving even potentially solvent financial institutions vulnerable to runs by their creditors, who were rattled and increasingly operating on a hair trigger.[8]

In a sense, no one should have been surprised by the turmoil. Unregulated and weakly regulated financial markets have historically shown a tendency toward excessive risk taking and instability. The reasons for this are worth reviewing.

To begin with, financial actors do not always bear the full consequences of their decisions and therefore are liable to take (or impose) more risk than would otherwise seem reasonable. For example, financial institutions generally invest other people's money and often enjoy asymmetric compensation incentives, which reward them for gains without penalizing them for losses. Even more troubling, the failure of a large financial firm can have systemic consequences, potentially triggering a cascade of losses, which means that risk taking by the firm can impose costs far beyond its own shareholders, creditors, and counterparties. The freezing up of the credit markets in 2008– 09, because even healthy banks are afraid to lend, is an especially serious example of this phenomenon.

A closely related problem is that of contagion or panic, in which fear drives a sudden surge in demand for safety and liquidity. A traditional bank run by depositors is one expression of contagion, but other types of creditors can also create a "run" on a financial institution and potentially weaken or destroy it; for example, short-term lenders can refuse to roll over existing loans to the institution, and market actors may refuse to continue to deal with it. In fact, whole markets can succumb to panic selling under certain circumstances. In all of these cases, the fearful depositors, creditors, and investors who suddenly decide to liquidate their positions may be imposing costs on others, since the first to run will generally get their money out whereas the last to do so typically will not. More broadly, poorly managed financial institutions impose costs on well-managed ones, because of the threat of contagion.

Yet another problem endemic to financial markets is that individual borrowers and investors may not always be ideally positioned to evaluate complex risks. How can any of us be sure that a particular financial agreement or product is safe? Ideally, we carefully read the contract or prospectus. But given limits on time and expertise (including the expense of expert advice), even a relatively careful consumer or investor is liable to make mistakes—and potentially large ones— from time to time. Virtually all of us, moreover, rely on various kinds of shortcuts in assessing risks in daily life—intuition, seeking nonexpert outside advice, a trusting attitude toward authority, and so on. Although such an approach may normally work well, it sometimes fails and is particularly subject to manipulation—for example, by aggressive (or even predatory) lenders. Such problems were an important contributor to the excesses and eventual implosion of subprime mortgage lending. In addition, particularly in recent years, it appears that even many of the most sophisticated investors—and perhaps even the credit rating agencies themselves—had trouble assessing the risks associated with a wide array of new and complex financial instruments. Complexity itself may therefore have contributed to the binge of risk taking that overtook the United States financial system in recent years.

Failure of public risk management

Ideally, state and federal regulators should have intervened to control the worst financial excesses and abuses long before the crisis took hold. Almost everyone now recognizes that the government serves as the nation's ultimate risk manager—as the lender, insurer, and spender of last resort—in times of crisis. But effective public risk management is critical in normal times as well, both to protect consumers and investors and to help prevent crises from developing in the first place.[9]

A good example involves bank regulation. Americans have faced recurrent banking crises as well as frequent bank suspensions and failures for much of the nation's history. The problem appeared to ease after the creation of the Federal Reserve in 1914 but then returned with a vengeance in 1930–33, when a spiraling panic nearly consumed the entire American banking system. All of this changed after the introduction of federal deposit insurance in June of 1933. Bank runs virtually disappeared, and bank failures fell sharply. Critics worried that the existence of federal insurance would encourage excessive risk taking (moral hazard), because depositors would no longer have to worry about the soundness of their banks and instead would be attracted by the higher interest rates that riskier banks offered. The authors of the 1933 legislation prepared for this threat, authorizing not only public deposit insurance but also intelligent bank regulation designed to ensure the safety and soundness of insured banks. The end result was an effective system of new consumer protections, a remarkable reduction in systemic risk, and a notable increase in public confidence in the financial system. By all indications, well-designed government risk management helped strengthen the market and prevent subsequent crises.[10] (See figure below: Bank Failures, 1864– 2000).

In our own time, appropriate regulatory measures might have proved similarly salutary. Reasonable controls on overly risky consumer and corporate lending and effective limits on the leverage of major (systemic) financial institutions might have been enough, by themselves, to prevent the worst aspects of the collapse. Greater regulatory attention in numerous other areas, from money market funds and credit rating agencies to credit default swaps, might also have made a positive difference. However, key policymakers, particularly at the federal level, often chose not to expand this critical risk-management role—to cover new and emerging risks—when they had the chance.

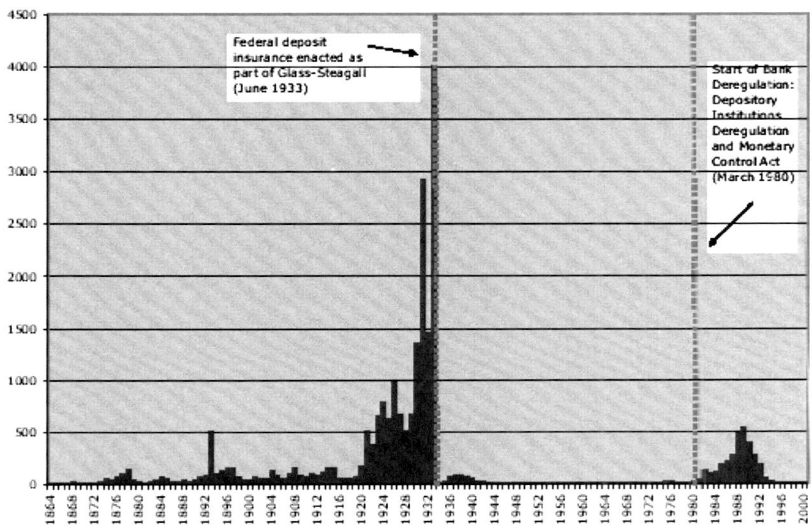

Source: David Moss, "An Ounce of Prevention: The Power of Sound Risk Management in Stabilizing the American Financial System," 2009.

A Unique Period of Calm Amid the Storm: Bank Failures (Suspensions), 1864–2000

Looking forward, the need for meaningful regulatory reform has now become particularly urgent— not only to correct past mistakes, but also to limit the likelihood and the impact of future crises and to control the moral hazard that is likely to flow from the recent profusion of federal bailouts and guaranties. If creditors, employees, and even shareholders of major financial institutions conclude that the federal government is likely to step in again in case of trouble (because of the systemic significance of their institutions), they may become even more lax about monitoring risk, leading to even greater excesses in the future. For this reason, the recent federal actions in support of the nation's largest financial institutions, involving more than $10 trillion in new federal guaranties, make effective regulation after the crisis even more vital. The example set in 1933—of pairing explicit public insurance with an effective regulatory mechanism for monitoring and controlling moral hazard—must not be forgotten. In fact, the need to control the moral hazard created by the current financial rescue may be the most important reason of all for strengthening financial regulation in the months and years ahead.

Failure to Require Sufficient Transparency

While allowing financial institutions to take on too much risk, federal and state regulators at the same time have permitted these actors to provide too little information to protect investors and enable markets to function honestly and efficiently. Because financial information often represents a public good, it may not be adequately provided in the marketplace without government encouragement or mandate. Investors without access to basic financial reporting face serious information asymmetries, potentially raising the cost of capital and compromising the efficient allocation of financial resources.[11] Truthful disclosures are also essential to protect investors. Essential disclosure and reporting requirements may therefore enhance efficiency by reducing these informational asymmetries. The broad availability of financial information also promises to boost public confidence in financial markets. As former Securities and Exchange Commssion (SEC) Chairman Arthur Levitt has observed, "the success of capital is directly dependent on the quality of accounting and disclosure systems. Disclosure systems that are founded on high-quality standards give investors confidence in the credibility of financial reporting—and without investor confidence, markets cannot thrive."[12]

From the time they were introduced at the federal level in the early 1930s, disclosure and reporting requirements have constituted a defining feature of American securities regulation (and of American financial regulation more generally). President Franklin Roosevelt himself explained in April 1933 that although the federal government should never be seen as endorsing or promoting a private security, there was "an obligation upon us to insist that every issue of new securities to be sold in interstate commerce be accompanied by full publicity and information and that no essentially important element attending the issue shall be concealed from the buying public."[13]

Historically, embedding a flexible approach to jurisdiction has made for strong, effective regulatory agencies. When the SEC was founded, during the Depression, Congress armed the commission with statutory authority based upon an extremely broad view of what constituted a security and gave it wide latitude in determining what disclosures were necessary from those who sought to sell securities to the public. There was a similar breadth of coverage and flexibility in substantive approach in the Investment Advisors Act and the Investment Company Act, which together governed money managers. These broad grants of jurisdiction led to the SEC's having regulatory authority over most capital-market transactions outside the banking and insurance systems until the end of the 1970s.

However, the financial markets have outpaced even the broadest grants of regulatory authority. Starting in the 1980s, skilled market operators began to exploit what had previously seemed to be merely insignificant loopholes in this system—exceptions that had always existed in the regulation of investment management. The increasing importance of institutional intermediaries in the capital markets exacerbated this tendency. By the 1990s, the growth of over-the-counter derivative markets had created unregulated parallel capital-market products. This trend has continued in recent years, with the SEC allowing the founding of publicly traded hedge-fund and private-equity management firms that do not have to register as investment companies.

Over subsequent years, the reach of the SEC and its reporting requirements were gradually expanded. Securities traded over the counter, for example, were brought into the fold beginning in 1964. The SEC targeted "selective disclosure" in 2000 with Regulation Fair Disclosure (Reg FD), a new weapon in the ongoing fight against insider activities. Two years later, Congress passed the Sarbanes-Oxley Act, which aimed to bolster the independence of the accounting industry and required top corporate executives to personally certify key financial statements.[14]

By the time the crisis struck in 2007–08, however, one of the most common words used to describe the American financial system was "opaque." Hedge funds, which squeeze into an exemption in the Investment Company Act of 1940, face almost no registration or reporting requirements; moreover, a modest attempt by the SEC to change this situation was struck down in federal court in 2006. Similarly, over-the-counter markets for credit default swaps and other derivative instruments remain largely unregulated and, say critics, constitute virtually the polar opposite of open and transparent exchange. (According to news reports, an attempt by Brooksley Born, the former chairperson of the Commodity Futures Trading Commission, to regulate OTC-traded derivatives in 1997–98, was blocked by Fed Chairman Alan Greenspan, Treasury Secretary Robert Rubin, and others, allegedly on the grounds that such regulation could precipitate a financial crisis. In any event, Congress in 2000 prohibited regulation of most derivatives.)[15] In addition, the proliferation of off-balance-sheet entities (conduits, structured investment vehicles [SIVs], etc.) and the rapid growth of highly complex financial instruments (such as CDOs) further undermined clarity and understanding in the marketplace. The financial consultant Henry Kaufman maintains that leading financial institutions actively "pushed legal structures that made many aspects of the financial markets opaque."[16] Moreover, starting in 1994, with the Central Bank of Denver decision,[17] the courts have severely limited the ability of investors to police transparency failures involving financial institutions working with public companies. This failure was extended in the Supreme Court's Stoneridge decision,[18] closing off liability to investors even in cases in which financial institutions were participants in a fraudulent scheme.

There are of course legitimate questions about how far policymakers should go in requiring disclosure—where the line should be drawn between public and proprietary information. But particularly given the breakdown that has now occurred, it is difficult to escape the conclusion that America's financial markets have veered far from the goal of transparency, fundamentally compromising the health and vitality of the financial sector and, ultimately, the whole economy.

Why our regulatory system failed to expand the zone of transparency in the face of far-reaching financial innovation is a question that merits careful attention. At least part of the answer, once again, appears to be that key regulators preferred not to expand the regulatory system to address these challenges, or simply believed that such expansion was unnecessary. In 2002, for example, Federal Reserve Chairman Alan Greenspan explained his view on "the issue of regulation and disclosure in the over-the-counter derivatives market" this way:

> By design, this market, presumed to involve dealings among sophisticated professionals, has been largely exempt from government regulation. In part, this exemption reflects the view that professionals do not require the investor protections commonly afforded to markets in which retail investors participate. But regulation is not only unnecessary in these markets, it is potentially damaging, because regulation presupposes disclosure and forced disclosure of proprietary information can undercut innovations in financial markets just as it would in real estate markets.[19]

Subsequent developments—including the effective failure (and rescue) of American International Group, Inc. (AIG), as a result of massive exposure in the credit default swaps market—raise serious questions about this hands-off view. The abuses in the mortgage markets, and especially in the subprime mortgage market, are a good example, but so are abuses throughout the range of consumer credit products. The challenge now is to develop a plan not only to bring much-needed sunlight into the most opaque corners of the financial system but to ensure appropriate regulatory adaptation to new financial innovation in the future.

Failure to Ensure Fair Dealings

The current regulatory system has not only allowed for excessive risk and an insufficient degree of transparency, but it has also failed to prevent the emergence of unfair dealings between actors. Overt lies are dishonest, of course, and lying may trigger legal liability. But fair dealing involves more than refraining from outright lying. Deception and misdirection are the antithesis of fair dealing. When the legal system permits deception and misdirection it undermines consensual agreements between parties, the very foundation of a market economy designed to serve all individuals.

Deceptive or misleading dealings can occur in any setting, but they are most likely to occur when the players are mismatched. When one player is sophisticated, has ample resources, and works regularly in the field while the other is a nonspecialist with limited resources and little experience, the potential for deception is at its highest. A credit card contract, for example, may be a relatively simple, straightforward agreement from which both issuer and customer may benefit. Or it may be a thirty-plus page document that is virtually incomprehensible to the customer. In the latter case, the issuer who can hire a team of lawyers to draft the most favorable language may carefully measure every nuance of the transaction, while the customer who has little time or sufficient expertise to read—much less negotiate—such a contract is far less likely to appreciate the risks associated with the deal.

Similarly, in the subprime mortgage market prospective borrowers were often led to believe that a scheduled interest-rate reset would never affect them because they had been told that they could "always" refinance the property at a lower rate before the reset took effect. Similarly, studies show that payday loan customers, while generally aware of finance charges, are often unaware of annual percentage rates.[20] In one survey, of those who took on tax refund anticipation loans, approximately half of all respondents were not aware of the substantial fees charged by the lender.[21] One authority on consumer credit has catalogued a long list of "tricks and traps," particularly in the credit card market, designed to "catch consumers who stumble or mistake those traps for treasure and find themselves caught in a snare from which they cannot escape."[22] While each of these contracts may meet the letter of the law, deals that are structured so that one side repeatedly does not understand the terms do not meet the definition of fair dealing.

The available evidence suggests that the costs of deceptive financial products are high, quickly climbing into the billions of dollars annually. 23 But the problem is not limited to monetary loss— many people are stripped not only of their wealth, but also of their confidence in the financial marketplace. They come to regard all financial products with suspicion, including those on fair terms and those that could be beneficial to them.

As the recent crisis has shown, the effects of deceptive contracts can have wide ripple effects. For example, deceptive mortgages have led to lender foreclosures on residential housing—foreclosures that cost taxpayers money and threaten the economic stability of already imperiled neighborhoods.[24] A recent housing report observed: "Foreclosures are costly—not only to homeowners, but also to a wide variety of stakeholders, including mortgage servicers, local governments and neighboring homeowners . . . up to $80,000 for all stakeholders combined."[25] Lenders can lose as well, forfeiting as much as $50,000 per foreclosure, which translates to roughly $25 billion in total foreclosure- related losses in 2003.[26] A city can lose up to $19,227 per house abandoned in foreclosure in lost property taxes, unpaid utility bills, property upkeep, sewage, and maintenance.[27] Many foreclosure- related costs fall on taxpayers, who ultimately must shoulder the bill for services provided by their local governments.

The burdens of credit-market imperfections are not spread evenly across economic, educational, or racial groups. The wealthy tend to be insulated from many credit traps, while the vulnerability of the working class and middle-class increases. For those closer to the economic margins, a single economic mistake—a credit card with an interest rate that unexpectedly escalates to 29.99 percent or misplaced trust in a broker who recommends a high-priced mortgage—can trigger a downward economic spiral from which no recovery is possible. There is ample evidence that African Americans and Hispanics have been targets for certain deceptive products, much to their injury and to the injury of a country that prizes equality of opportunity for all its citizens.[28]

When businesses sell deceptive products, they not only injure their customers but also injure their competitors, who are forced to adopt similar practices or face losing their markets. The result is a downward spiral, a race to the bottom in which those who offer the most slyly deceptive products enjoy the greatest profits while entire industries and markets are corrupted and cease to provide efficient and mutually beneficial transactions. The same phenomenon operates on a more macroeconomic level: some investment banks that may have had initial doubts about packing subprime loans were drawn into a downward spiral, abandoning their standards of investment quality in a race for the same profits that other firms appeared to be making.

Assuring fair dealing is not the same as assuring that no one makes a mistake. Buyers and sellers of financial services can miscalculate. They can fail to save, take unwise gambles, or simply buy too much. Personal responsibility will always play a critical role in dealing with financial products, just as personal responsibility remains essential to the responsible use of any physical product. Fair dealing assures only that deception and misdirection will not bring a person to ruin, while it leaves room to maximize the opportunities for people to chart their own economic futures, free to succeed and free to fail.

The government can play a unique role in assuring that repeat dealings in circumstances of substantial imbalances of power and knowledge are nonetheless fair dealings. Regulation can assure a more level playing field, one in which the terms of an agreement, for example, are clear and easily understood. When terms are clear, individuals are more likely to compare options, which in turn drives far greater market efficiency. More importantly, when terms are clear, individuals are better able to assess investment risks and are thus empowered to make decisions that are more beneficial for themselves.

By limiting the opportunities for deception and allowing for the necessary trust to develop between interconnected parties, regulation can enhance the vitality of financial markets. Historically, new regulation has often served this role. For example, as the money manager Martin Whitman has observed, far from stifling the markets, the new regulations of the Investment Company Act of 1940 enabled the targeted industry to flourish:

> It ill behooves any successful money manager in the mutual fund industry to condemn the very strict regulation embodied in the Investment Company Act of 1940. Without strict regulation, I doubt that our industry could have grown as it has grown, and also be as prosperous as it is for money managers. Because of the existence of strict regulation, the outside investor knows that money managers can be trusted. Without that trust, the industry likely would not have grown the way it has grown.[29]

Markets built on fair dealing produce benefits for all Americans on both sides of the transactions.

3. The Central Importance of Regulatory Philosophy

The magnitude of the current financial crisis makes clear that America's system of financial regulation has failed. As a result, there is now growing interest in reforming the essential structure of financial regulation in the United States. (See the appendix for a summary of other recent reports on regulatory reform.) Critics highlight the inherent problems of vesting regulatory authority in a large number of separate agencies at both the state and federal levels, each responsible for isolated elements of a vast financial architecture. Although this complex regulatory system benefits from competition across governmental bodies, it also suffers from the problem of "regulatory arbitrage" (a situation in which regulated firms play regulators off against one another) as well as numerous gaps in coverage.

Structural and organizational problems are certainly important, and are taken up in section III, below. But at root, the regulatory failure that gave rise to the current crisis was one of philosophy more than structure. In too many cases, regulators had the tools but failed to use them. And where tools were missing, regulators too often failed to ask for the necessary authority to develop what was needed.

Markets are powerful and robust institutions, and a healthy respect for free market activity has served this nation well since its founding. At the same time, the best tradition in American policy has always been pragmatic. History has consistently shown that markets cannot be counted upon to regulate themselves or to function efficiently in the absence of regulation. While the price mechanism calibrates supply and demand, it cannot prevent bank runs, abusive lending or Ponzi schemes without regulation. The current financial meltdown proves these points in an especially severe way.

Excesses and abuse are all too common in a system without regulation. Government thus has a vital role to play. As President Lincoln once wrote: "The legitimate object of government, is to do for a community of people, whatever they need to have done, but can not do, *at all*, or can not, *so well do*, for themselves—in their separate, and individual capacities."[30]

Lincoln's vision of government goes beyond correcting abuses to improving the welfare of "a community of people." Regulators must never lose sight of the fact that the well-being of Americans is their goal, and that the welfare of the people has never been best served by extreme political ideologies. Franklin Roosevelt perhaps put it best: the question, he said, is "whether individual men and women will have to serve some system of government or economics, or whether a system of government and economics exists to serve individual men and women."[31] Not only is this pragmatic approach democratic, asking regulation and the market to serve the American people, but it also places the American people at the foundation of the economy. If Americans are secure and flourishing, the financial system will be secure and flourishing as well. If Americans are in crisis or face considerable risks, so too will the financial system. Success is defined by the quality of life Americans have, not by the impersonal metrics of any theory of government or economics.

Well-conceived financial regulation has the potential not only to safeguard markets against excesses and abuse but also to strengthen markets as foundations of innovation and growth. Creativity and innovation are too often channeled into circumventing regulation and exploiting loopholes. Smart financial regulations can redirect creative energy from these unproductive endeavors to innovations that increase efficiency and address the tangible risks people face. 32 As discussed above, the decades following the New Deal regulatory reforms were the longest period without a serious finanial crisis in the nation's history; they were also a period of unusually high average real economic growth.

In April 2008, former Federal Reserve Chairman Paul Volcker commented on these developments in a speech to the Economic Club of New York:

> [T]oday's financial crisis is the culmination, as I count them, of at least five serious breakdowns of systemic significance in the past twenty-five

> years—on the average one every five years. Warning enough that something rather basic is amiss.
>
> Over that time, we have moved from a commercial bank–centered, highly regulated financial system, to an enormously more complicated and highly engineered system. Today, much of the financial intermediation takes place in markets beyond effective official oversight and supervision, all enveloped in unknown trillions of derivative instruments. It has been a highly profitable business, with finance accounting recently for 35 to 40 percent of all corporate profits.
>
> It is hard to argue that the new system has brought exceptional benefits to the economy generally. Economic growth and productivity in the last twenty-five years has been comparable to that of the 1950s and '60s, but in the earlier years the prosperity was more widely shared.
>
> The sheer complexity, opaqueness, and systemic risks embedded in the new markets—complexities and risks little understood even by most of those with management responsibilities—has enormously complicated both official and private responses to this current mother of all crises....
>
> Simply stated, the bright new financial system—for all its talented participants, for all its rich rewards—has failed the test of the market place....
>
> In sum, it all adds up to a clarion call for an effective response.[33]

As Volcker himself went on to observe, there is no going back to the "heavily regulated, bank dominated, nationally insulated markets" of the past.[34] At the same time, given the enormity of the current crisis and the evident failure of financial markets to regulate themselves, it is imperative that Congress take up the challenge of fashioning appropriate regulation for the twenty-first century—to stabilize and strengthen the nation's financial markets in the face of extraordinary innovation and globalization. For this to work, we must first remind ourselves that government has a vital role to play, not in replacing financial markets or overwhelming them with rules, but in bolstering financial markets through judicious regulation. Rooted in the principles of sound risk management, transparency, and fairness, new financial regulation can succeed, and must succeed.

IV. Critical Problems and Recommendations for Improvement

The sweeping nature of the current financial crisis points to the need for a thorough review of financial regulation and, ultimately, for significant regulatory reform. As discussed in part III, financial regulation is particularly necessary to manage risk, facilitate transparency, and ensure fair dealings. The current system has failed on all counts, and as a result, numerous discrete problems have emerged. This report focuses on the following most critical of these problems:

1. Systemic risk is often not identified or regulated until crisis is imminent.
2. Many financial institutions carry dangerous amounts of leverage.
3. The unregulated "shadow financial system" is a source of significant systemic risk.
4. Ineffective regulation of mortgages and other consumer credit products produces unfair, and often abusive, treatment of consumers, but also creates risks for lending institutions and the financial system.
5. Executive pay packages incentivize excessive risk.
6. The credit rating system is ineffective and plagued with conflicts of interest.
7. The globalization of financial markets encourages countries to compete to attract foreign capital by offering increasingly permissive regulatory laws that increase market risk.
8. Participants, observers, and regulators neither predicted nor developed contingency plans to address the current crisis.

This section addresses each problem in turn, and provides recommendations for improvement.

1. Identify and Regulate Financial Institutions That Pose Systemic Risk

Problem with current system: **Systemic risk is often not identified or regulated until crisis is imminent.**

Today, there is no regulator with the authority to determine which financial institutions or products pose a systemic risk to the broader economy. In 2008, Bear Stearns, Fannie Mae, Freddie Mac, AIG, and Citigroup all appear to have been deemed too big—or, more precisely, too deeply embedded in the financial system—to fail. The decisions to rescue these institutions were often made in an ad hoc fashion by regulators with no clear mandate to act nor the proper range of financial tools with which to act.

This is the wrong approach. Systemic risk needs to be managed before moments of crisis, by regulators who have clear authority and the proper tools. Once a crisis has arisen, financial regulation has already failed. The underlying problem can no longer be prevented, it can only be managed, often at the cost of extraordinary expenditures of taxpayer dollars.

Action item: **Mandate that a new or existing agency or an interagency task force regulate systemic risk within the financial system on an ongoing basis.**

A much better approach would be to identify the degree of systemic risk posed by financial institutions, products, and markets in advance—that is, in normal times—and to regulate them accordingly. Providing proper oversight of such institutions would help to prevent a crisis from striking in the first place, and it would put public officials in a much better position to deal with the consequences should a crisis occur.[35]

To make this possible, Congress and the President should designate a body charged with identifying the degree of systemic risk posed by financial institutions, products, and markets. This body could be an existing agency, such as the Board of Governors of the Federal Reserve System, a new agency, or a coordinating body of existing regulators.[36]

The need for a body to identify and regulate institutions with systemic significance is a necessary response to two clear lessons of the current financial crisis: (1) systemic risk is caused by institutions that are not currently covered or adequately covered by the financial services regulatory system; and (2) in a crisis the federal government may feel compelled to stabilize systemically significant institutions. However, no regulatory body currently has the power to identify and regulate systemically significant nonbank institutions. Consequently, Congress should authorize legitimate, coherent governmental powers and processes for doing so.

The systemic regulator should have the authority to require reporting of relevant information from all institutions that may be systemically significant or engaged in systemically significant activities. It should have a process for working with the regulatory bodies charged with the day-to-day oversight of the financial system. Finally, it should have clear authority and the proper tools for addressing a systemic crisis.

The regulator should operate according to the philosophy that systemic risk is a product of the interaction of institutions and products with market conditions. Thus, the regulator would oversee structures described in the next two action items that address a continuum of systemic risk by increasing capital and insurance requirements as financial institutions grow. This approach seeks to maximize the incentives for private parties to manage risk while recognizing and acting upon the fact that as financial institutions grow they become more "systemically significant."

Finally, creating a systemic risk regulator is not a substitute for ongoing regulation of our capital markets, focused on safety and soundness, transparency, and accountability. The agencies charged with those missions must be strengthened while we at the same time address the problem of systemic risk.

Action item: **Impose heightened regulatory requirements for systemically significant institutions to reduce the risk of financial crisis.**

Precisely because of the potential threat they pose to the broader financial system, systemically significant institutions should face enhanced prudential regulation to limit excessive risk taking and help ensure their safety. Such regulation might include relatively stringent capital and liquidity requirements, most likely on a countercyclical basis; an overall maximum leverage ratio (on the whole institution and potentially also on individual subsidiaries); well-defined limits on contingent liabilities and off-balance-sheet activity; and perhaps also caps on the proportion of short-term debt on the institution's balance sheet. The systemic regulator should consider the desirability of capping any taxpayer guarantee and whether to require systemically significant firms to purchase federal capital insurance under which the bank, in return for a premium payment, would receive a certain amount of capital in specified situations.[37]

Whether such enhanced oversight for systemically significant institutions should be provided by a new systemic regulator or by existing regulatory agencies is a question that requires further study and deliberation.

Action item: **Establish a receivership and liquidation process for systemically significant nonbank institutions that is similar to the system for banks.**

The current bankruptcy regime under the Bankruptcy Code does not work well for systemically significant nonbanks institutions. Recent experience with the failure of Bear Stearns & Co. and Lehman Brothers Inc. has indicated that there are gaps in the system for handling the receivership or liquidation of systemically significant financial institutions that are not banks or broker-dealers and are therefore subject to the Bankruptcy Code. Two problems are evident: (1) Because the federal bankruptcy system was not designed for a large, systemically significant financial institution, financial regulators may feel the need to prop up the ailing institution in order to avoid a messy and potentially destructive bankruptcy process, and (2) the Bankruptcy Code's provisions for distribution of the assets of a bankrupt financial institution do not take into account the systemic considerations that regulators are obligated to consider.

The Panel recommends that systemically significant nonbank financial institutions be made subject to a banklike receivership and liquidation scheme. We note that the bankruptcy regime under the Federal Deposit Insurance Act has generally worked well.

2. Limit Excessive Leverage in American Financial Institutions

Problem with current system: **Excessive leverage carries substantial risks for financial institutions.**

Leverage within prudent limits is a valuable financial tool. But excessive leverage in the financial sector is dangerous and can pose a significant risk to the financial system. In fact, it is now widely believed that overleveraging (i.e., relying on an increasingly steep ratio of borrowing to capital) at key financial institutions helped to convert the initial subprime turmoil in 2007 into a full-blown financial crisis in 2008.

Recent estimates suggest that just prior to the crisis, investment banks and securities firms, hedge funds, depository institutions, and the government-sponsored mortgage enterprises (primarily Fannie Mae and Freddie Mac) held assets worth nearly $23 trillion on a base of $1.9 trillion in capital, yielding an overall average leverage ratio of approximately 12:1. We must, however, consider this figure carefully, because average leverage varied widely for different types of financial institutions. The most heavily leveraged, as a class, were broker-dealers and hedge funds, with an average leverage ratio of 27:1; government sponsored enterprises were next, with an average ratio of 23.5:1.35. Commercial banks were toward the low end, with an average ratio of 9.8:1, and savings banks have the lowest average ratio at 8.7:1.

Financial institutions pursue leverage for numerous reasons. All bank lending, for example, is leveraged, because a certain amount of capital is permitted to support a much larger volume of loans. And the leverage of financial institutions is generally procyclical, meaning that it tends to increase when asset prices are rising (when leverage seems safer) and tends to decline when they are falling (when leverage seems more dangerous).[38]

For an institution with high debt and a relatively small base of capital, returns on equity are greatly magnified. Unfortunately, high leverage can also prove destabilizing because it effectively magnifies losses as well as gains. If a firm with $10 billion in assets is leveraged 10:1, then a loss of just 3 percent ($300 million) on total assets translates into a 30 percent decline in capital (from $1 billion to $700 million), raising the bank's leverage ratio to nearly 14:1. The challenge is obviously far more extreme for a firm with leverage of 30:1, as was typical for leading investment banks prior to the crisis. Here, a 3 percent ($300 million) loss on total assets translates into a 90-percent decline in capital (from $333 million to $33 million) and a new leverage ratio of nearly 300:1. To get back to leverage of 30:1, that firm would either have to raise $300 million in new equity (to bring capital back to its original level) or collapse its balance sheet, selling more than 95 percent ($9.37 billion) of its assets and paying off an equivalent amount of debt.[39]

Although raising $300 million in new equity would seem vastly preferable to selling $9.37 billion in assets, the problem is that financial institutions with depleted capital often find it difficult to raise new equity, particularly in times of general financial distress. If sufficient new capital is not available and the weakened firms are ultimately forced to dispose of assets under firesale conditions, this can depress asset prices further, generating additional losses across the financial system (particularly in the context of mark-to-market accounting). In the extreme, these sales can set off a vicious downward spiral of forced selling, falling prices, rising losses and, in turn, more forced selling.

***Action item:* Adopt one or more regulatory options to strengthen risk-based capital and curtail leverage.**

The goal of enhanced capital requirements is to limit excessive risk taking during boom times and reducing the need for dangerous "fire sales" during downturns. Several common criteria must be met by proposals for enhanced capital requirements. Above all, any such proposals must operate in a way that does not restrict prudent leverage or produce other unintended consequences. Moreover, they must recognize that proper risk adjustment can prove particularly vexing: the appropriateness of a leverage ratio depends on the safety of the assets the leverage supports, both directly and in the context of the business as a whole. Determining that safety level is anything but easy, as the current crisis shows. Finally, any proposal must recognize that no one solution will fit the entire financial sector (or perhaps even all institutions of one type within the financial sector).

A number of valuable ideas have been proposed as ways to strengthen capital and curtail excessive leverage, including the following:

Objectives-based capital requirements

Under this approach, capital requirements should be applied not simply according to the type of institution (commercial bank, broker-dealer, hedge fund, etc.) but on the basis of regulatory objectives (for example, guard against systemic risk, etc.). For example, required capital ratios could be made to increase progressively with the size of the firm's balance sheet, so that larger financial institutions face a lower limit on leverage than smaller ones (on the assumption that larger firms have greater systemic implications and ultimately become "too big to fail"). Required capital ratios could also be made to vary with other variables that regulators determine to be salient, such as the proportion of short-term debt on an institution's balance sheet or the identity of the holders of its liabilities.

Leverage requirements

Beyond risk-based capital requirements, there is also a strong argument for unweighted capital requirements, to control overall leverage. Stephen Morris and Hyun Song Shin suggest that these "leverage requirements" are necessary to limit systemic risk, by reducing the need for dangerous asset fire sales in a downturn.[40] FDIC Chairperson Sheila Bair has been particularly insistent on this point, declaring in 2006, for example, that "the leverage ratio—a simple tangible capital to assets measure—is a critically important component of our regulatory capital regime."[41] It should be noted that the current crisis may be exacerbated because leverage ratios are not a common feature of banking regulation in Europe; any approach to curtailing leverage in a globalized financial system must implement such standards on a global basis.

Countercyclical capital requirements

To help financial institutions prepare for the proverbial rainy day and manage effectively in a downturn, it has been proposed that capital (and provisioning) requirements be made countercyclical—that is, more stringent when asset prices are rising and less stringent when they are falling. Since the procyclicality of financial institution leverage likely intensifies the ups and downs in asset markets, countercyclical capital requirements could serve as a valuable automatic stabilizer, effectively leaning against the wind. One approach could involve a framework that raises capital adequacy requirements by a ratio linked to the growth of the value of bank's assets in order to tighten lending and build up reserves when times are good. Spain's apparently favorable experience with "dynamic provisioning" in its banking regulation serves as a model for many related proposals.[42] Joseph Stiglitz takes the idea one step further, suggesting that a "simple regulation would have prevented a large fraction of the crises around the world—speed limits restricting the rate at which banks can expand, say, their portfolio of loans. Very rapid rates of expansion are typically a sign of inadequate screening."[43] Similarly, because rapid increases in leverage appear to precede periods of financial turmoil, capital requirements could be tailored to discourage particularly quick buildups of leverage.

Liquidity requirements

To further address the problem of financial firms being forced to sell illiquid assets into a falling market, some commentators have proposed that regulators could impose liquidity requirements in addition to capital requirements, so that financial firms would have to hold a certain proportion of liquid assets as well as a liquidity buffer that could be used in a crisis. Armed with sufficient supply of liquid assets (such as treasury bills), firms could safely sell these assets in a downturn without placing downward pressure on the prices of less liquid assets, which would contribute to systemic risk.[44]

These and other proposals will need to be thoughtfully reviewed, bearing in mind that leverage is not a consistent phenomenon, but rather varies across financial institutions, regulatory structures, and different types of leveraged situations. The current crisis provides two lessons to inform this review. First, options to curtail excessive leverage must proceed as a top priority and an integral part of the restructuring of the regulation of American financial institutions. Second, reforms in this area must reflect the primary lesson of the crisis: that no asset types, however labeled, and no transaction patterns, however familiar, are inherently stable.

3. Modernize Supervision of Shadow Financial System

***Problem with current system:* The unregulated "shadow financial system" is a source of significant systemic risk.**

Since 1990, certain large markets and market intermediary institutions have developed outside the jurisdiction of financial market regulators. Collectively, these markets and market actors have become known as the shadow financial system.[45] The key components of the shadow financial system are unregulated financial instruments such as over-the-counter (OTC) derivatives, offbalance-sheet entities such as conduits and SIVs,[46] and nonbank institutions such as hedge funds and private equity funds. While the shadow financial system must be brought within any plan for systemic risk management, that alone would be insufficient. Routine disclosure-based capital- market regulation and routine safety-and-soundness regulation of financial institutions will not function effectively unless regulators have jurisdiction over the shadow financial system and are able to enforce common standards of transparency, accountability, and adequate capital reserves.

As a result of the growth of the shadow financial system, it is nearly impossible for regulators or the public to understand the real dynamics of either bank credit markets or public capital markets. This became painfully clear during the collapse of Bear Stearns and the subsequent bankruptcy of Lehman Brothers, and the collapse of AIG. In the case of Bear Stearns, key regulators expressed the view that as a result of that firm's extensive dealing with hedge funds and in the derivatives markets, the systemic threat posed by a disorderly bankruptcy could prove quite severe, though difficult to predict with any certainty. [47] Six months later, Lehman Brothers was allowed to file for protection under Chapter 11, the only major financial firm to be allowed to do in the United States during the financial crisis. Lehman's bankruptcy resulted in substantial systemwide disruption, particularly as a result of credit default swap obligations triggered by Lehman's default on its debt obligations. The unregulated nature of several financial markets involved in this crisis contributed to the inability of regulators to understand the unfolding problems and act responsively.

***Action item*: Ensure consistency of regulation for instruments currently operating in the shadow financial system.**

Extending the reach of financial regulation to cover the shadow financial system is necessary in order to accurately measure and manage risk across the markets. A consistent regulatory regime will also reduce the ability of market players to escape regulation by using complex financial instruments and to secure higher yields by masking risk through information asymmetries.

The Panel urges Congress to consider shifting the focus of existing regulation toward a functional approach. While the details would need to be worked out by empowered regulators, the principle is simple: hedge funds and private equity funds are money managers and should be regulated according to the same principles that govern the regulation of money managers generally. At a minimum, Congress must grant the SEC the clear authority to require hedge fund advisors to register as investment advisors under the Investment Advisors Act. If they venture into writing insurance contracts or providing credit to others, hedge funds' activities in these areas need to be regulated according to the principles governing insurance or lending. An over-the-counter derivative can be almost any kind of contract synthesizing almost any kind of economic act—such instruments need to be regulated according to what they do, not what they are called.

While further study is needed, proposals for regulating more consistently instruments currently in the shadow financial system include: applying capital requirements to firms engaged in making credit or insurance commitments through derivatives; requiring transparency around derivatives contracts tied to publicly traded securities; and holding hedge funds and private equity funds to a single, well-understood federal standard of fiduciary duty as other money managers are. However, regulating the shadow markets does not necessarily mean treating a hedge fund in the same manner as a mutual fund, or a credit default swap between institutions in the same manner as an insurance policy sold to retail consumers. Functional regulation can mean applying the same principles and not necessarily producing identical regulatory outcomes.

***Action item:* Increase transparency in OTC derivatives markets.**

The Panel also recommends implementing new measures to improve transparency in the shadow financial system. Lack of transparency in the shadow financial system contributed to failures of risk management and difficulty in pricing assets and assessing the health of financial institutions. Transparency can be enhanced in several ways; several options are presented below:

Regulated clearinghouses

A clearinghouse is an entity that provides clearance and settlement services with respect to financial products. It acts as a central counterparty with respect to trades that it clears. When the original parties to the trade introduce it to the clearinghouse for clearing, the original trade is replaced by two new trades in which the clearinghouse becomes the buyer to the original seller and the seller to the original buyer.

Proposals for clearinghouses generally involve the clearinghouse itself taking on credit risk. Such credit risk raises the issue of how to provide adequate capital in case of a default. One method for doing so involves taking the "margin" to secure performance of each trade. Another method involves daily marks-to-market to reduce risk arising from price fluctuations in the value of the contract. Others have proposed guaranty funds, in which each of the clearing members of the clearinghouse puts up a deposit to cover its future liabilities. Most central counterparty proposals also involve "mutualization of risk," in which the guaranty fund deposits of all clearing members may be used to cover a default by one member if the defaulting member's margin payments and guaranty fund contribution are insufficient to cover the loss. Finally, a clearinghouse may have the right to call for further contributions from members to cover any losses.

In addition to regulators risk management principles, a clearinghouse structure may also involve inspection by federal for the purposes of detecting and punishing fraudulent activity and public reporting of prices, volumes and open interest. [48]

Exchange-traded derivatives

As an alternative to clearinghouses, regulators can require that all standardized—and standardizable—OTC derivatives contracts be traded on regulated derviatives markets. These markets would be governed by the same standards that guide designated contract markets under the Commodity Exchange Act (CEA). CEA-governed exchanges must fully disclose the terms of the contracts traded and rules governing trading, and must also publicly report prices, volumes and open interest. The exchange would maintain detailed records to be inspected by federal regulators and would be empowered with the ability to deter, detect, and punish fraudulent activity. Intermediaries participating in the exchange would face registration, reporting, and capital adequacy requirements as well. Finally, the exchanges could still make use of clearinghouses to minimize counterparty risk.

Public reporting requirements

SEC Chairman Christopher Cox has proposed requiring CDS market participants to adhere to a public disclosure regime that would allow regulators to monitor market risk and potential market abuse. Cox' s proposals include: (1) public reports of OTC transactions to improve transparency and pricing, and (2) reporting to the SEC derivatives positions that affect public securities.[49]

4. Create a New System for Federal and State Regulation of Mortgages and Other Consumer Credit Products

***Problem with current system:* Ineffective regulation of mortgages and other consumer credit products has produced unfair, and often abusive, treatment of consumers, which destabilizes both families and the financial institutions that trade in those products.**

For decades, default rates on traditional home mortgages were low; profits to mortgage lenders were steady. Millions of Americans used mortgages to enable them to buy homes and retain homes. Over time, however, a number of mortgage lenders and brokers began offering higher-priced, higherprofit—and higher risk—mortgages to millions of families.[50] Unlike the low-risk "prime" mortgages of the 1940s through the 1990s, the new "subprime" offered much bigger payouts for lenders and, ultimately, for the investors to whom the lenders sold these mortgages, but they also created higher costs and greater risks for consumers. For example, a family buying a $175,000 home with a subprime loan with an effective interest rate of 15.6 percent would pay an extra $420,000 during the 30-year life of the mortgage—that is, over and above the payments due on a prime 6.5 percent mortgage. While investors were attracted to the bigger returns associated with these subprime mortgages, many overlooked the much bigger risks of default that have now become glaringly apparent.

The new subprime mortgages were marked by exotic, and often predatory, new features, such as two year teaser rates that permitted marketing of mortgages to individuals who could not have qualified for credit at the enormous required rate increase in year three, or so-called "liars" or "nodoc" loans based on false paperwork about a borrower's financial situation. Terms such as these virtually guaranteed that the mortgages would default, and families would lose their homes, unless the real estate price inflation continued. These mortgages were especially cruel for new, especially lower-income, home buyers. The data show, however, that a substantial number of middle-income families (and even some upper-income families) with low default risk signed up for subprime loans that were far more expensive than the prime mortgages for which they qualified.

The complexity of subprime mortgage products made understanding the costs associated with an offered mortgage, let alone comparing several mortgage products, almost impossible. The high proportion of people with good credit scores who ended up with high-cost mortgages raises the specter that some portion of these consumers were not fully cognizant of the fact that they could have borrowed for much less.[51] This conclusion is further corroborated by studies showing that subprime mortgage prices cannot be fully explained by borrower-specific and loan-specific risk factors.[52] These difficulties were further exacerbated by sharp selling practices and delayed disclosure of relevant documents. Buyers were steered to overpriced mortgages by brokers or other agents who represented themselves as acting in the borrower's best interests, but who were taking commissions from subprime lenders to steer them to riskier mortgages.[53] In other cases, lenders would not make relevant documents available until the closing date. In all of these respects, the mortgage market simply failed consumers.

Although mortgage documents include a raft of legally-required disclosures, those disclosures are a long way from a meaningful understanding of the loan transaction—and a much longer distance from supporting competitive markets. Many of the same points can be made for credit cards and other consumer financial products. In all of these cases consumers have little access to the key information they need to make responsible decisions. The result is a market in which people fail to assess risks properly, over-pay, and get into financial trouble. As the current crisis shows, these effects are not confined to those who buy the credit products. The high risk that consumers could not pay back their loans was multiplied by the bundling and re-bundling of millions of the loans into asset-backed securities;. That rebundling, in turn, spread the risk further, to the investment portfolios of other financial institutions, pension funds, state and local governments, and other investors for whom such risk was not appropriate. Ultimately, the widespread marketing of high-cost, high-risk consumer products has contributed to the destabilizing of the entire economy.

If, for example, a home buyer had been required to demonstrate an ability to pay the long-term mortgage rate rather than the teaser rate, home owners—and the country—would have been spared the specter of millions of foreclosures when payment resets made the monthly payment unaffordable. Moreover it would have been impossible to offer flawed investment products based on such mortgages.

State regulators have a long history as the first-line of protection for consumers. For example, states first sounded the alarm against predatory lending and brought landmark enforcement actions against some of the biggest subprime lenders, including Household, Beneficial Finance, AmeriQuest, and Delta Funding. But states are sometimes pressured to offer no more consumer protection than is offered on the federal level so that financial firms do not leave their state regulator for a more favorable regulatory environment (taking the fee revenues they provide with them).[54] Moreover, the same competition for business that exists at the state level also exists at the federal level. Federal regulators face the possibility of losing business both to state regulators or to other federal regulatory agencies. At the federal level, this problem is exacerbated by direct financial considerations. The budgets of the OCC and OTS, for example, are derived from the number and size of the financial institutions they regulate, which means that a bank's threat to leave a regulator has meaningful consequences.[55] As Professor Arthur Wilmarth has testified, "Virtually the entire [Office of the Comptroller of the Currency] budget is funded by national bank fees, and the biggest national banks pay the highest assessment rates.... The OCC's unimpressive enforcement record is, unfortunately, consistent with its strong budgetary incentive in maintaining the loyalty of leading national banks."[56]

This has caused much of the regulatory scheme to come unraveled. State usury laws have eroded; according to recent research, at least 35 states have amended their usury laws to make it legal to charge annual interest rates exceeding 300 percent in connection with consumer credit products.[57] Many states were apparently also unwilling to deal with subprime mortgages. In 2006, fully half— 52 percent—of subprime mortgages originated with companies that were subject only to state regulation.[58] And now, as the mortgage crisis deepens, the National Association of Attorneys General has a highly visible working group on foreclosures, but only about half of the states participate.

In addition, the authority of the states to deal with consumer protection for credit products has been sharply limited by interpretations in federal law. First, the Supreme Court has ruled that the usury laws of a national bank's state of incorporation controlled its activities nationwide. The decision naturally produced the pressures for repeal of state usury protections noted above. Second, the Office of the Comptroller of the Currency and federal courts have interpreted the National Banking Act to pre-empt action by state regulators to apply state consumer protection laws to national banks or to operating subsidiaries of national banks; virtually all of the nation's large banks—and most of those receiving federal assistance under the TARP—are national banks. The OCC's action was prompted by the attempt of Georgia to apply its Fair Lending Act to all banks within its jurisdiction. Yet, despite promises to Congress and the states, federal regulators have made the problem worse by failing to provide any significant supervision or regulation of their own.[59]

Action item: **Eliminate federal pre-emption of application of state consumer protection laws to national banks.**

Preemption affects states' consumer protection initiatives in three main respects:

1. *Standards*: The ability of states to set consumer protection laws and the scope of coverage for those laws.

2. *Visitation*: The ability of states to examine financial institutions for compliance with consumer protection laws.

3. *Enforcement*: The ability of states to impose penalties for violations of consumer protection laws.

Visitation and enforcement are closely connected but distinct.

Given the critical role of state consumer protection, Congress should amend the National Banking Act to provide clearly that state consumer protection laws can apply to national banks and to reverse the holding that the usury laws of a national bank's state of incorporation govern that bank's operation through the nation.

Action item: **Create a single federal regulator for consumer credit products.**

The need for a uniform federal law to create a meaningful baseline of protections is clear. It is essential that one regulatory agency have the responsibility and accountability for drafting, implementing, and overseeing effective consumer credit product protection rules. Without a uniform set of minimum standards, regulatory arbitrage among state—and federal—regulators will continue. and no regulator or agency will have the authority and responsibility to protect consumers.

The new federal regulator must be responsible for establishing minimum standards for disclosure and transparency, reviewing consumer credit products (in a manner set by statute) in light of those standards to eliminate unfair practices, and promoting practices that encourage the responsible use of credit. This regulator should assure that consumers are not misled by the terms of the sales pitches for credit products and that they have the information needed to make informed and thoughtful purchasing decisions. The statement of purposes of the legislation creating the new agency, and the standards governing its actions, would include the need to balance consumer protection with the legitimate need of financial institutions to create fair products and maintain the flow of credit to the national economy.

Creation of a single federal regulator would produce a single, national floor for consumer financial products. Some state regulators might conclude that their citizens require better protection, and they might put other constraints on the institutions that want to do business in their states. This proposal leaves them free to do so. The regulatory agency simply assures that all Americans, regardless of where they live, can count on basic protection. Regulations that apply to all products of a certain kind—e.g., mortgages, credit cards, payday loans—without any exceptions are far more comprehensive than those based on the kind of institution that issued them—federally chartered, state charted, thrift, bank, etc. Because such baselines are inescapable, the impact of regulatory arbitrage is sharply undercut. A financial institution cannot escape the restrictions on mortgage disclosures, for example, by reincorporating from a federal bank to a state bank. Any issuer of home mortgages must meet the minimum federal standards.

One option is to make the new federal regulator an independent agency within the financial regulatory community. This approach would have several advantages. A single regulator would have the opportunity to develop significant expertise in consumer products. Consumer protection would be a priority rather than one issue among many competing with a myriad of other regulatory priorities that have consistently commanded more attention in financial institution regulatory agencies. An agency devoted to consumer protection can make it a first priority to understand the functioning of financial products in the consumer marketplace. Expertise can also be concentrated from around the country. A single group of regulators can develop greater expertise to ensure that products are comprehensible to customers and that they are protected from unfair business practices. Such expertise can also be transferred from one product to another. As financial products become more functionally intertwined—for example, home equity lines of credit that operate like credit cards—an agency can develop the needed cross-expertise and more nuanced rules.

Another option is to place the new regulator within the Federal Reserve Board. The Board is the umbrella supervisor of bank holding companies, and it directly supervises state-chartered banks that choose to become members of the Federal Reserve System. It was given specific authority to deal with deceptive mortgages more than forty years ago. [60] Congress voted repeatedly to expand the Board's power to provide stronger consumer protection. [61]

Placing the new regulator within the Board would keep safety and soundness and consumer protection responsibilities together, on the ground that each responsibility, if properly implemented, could complement and re-enforce the other. Choosing that option, however, would require changes to the Federal Reserve Act to make consumer protection one of the Fed's primary responsibilities, on a par with bank supervision. It would also depend on a new understanding and attitude by the Board toward its execution of its consumer protection mission.

Federal Reserve Chairman Ben Bernanke has acknowledged that although the powers of the Fed to deal with mortgage abuses were "broad," [62] the Board has for years been slow to act,'[63] and the actions it took were inadequate.[64] Its power under TILA and HOEPA to issue regulations binding upon all mortgage lenders gave it the capacity to halt the lending practices that inflated the housing bubble and that lead millions of home owners toward eventual foreclosure, but the Fed failed to do so.

Similarly, in areas such as credit card regulation, only when Congress threatened to take away powers, did the Fed finally act.[65] Barney Frank, Chairman of the House Financial Services Committee, explained that the failure of the Fed to act was longstanding: "When Chairman Bernanke testified before us a few weeks ago . . . he said something I hadn't heard in my 28 years in this body, a Chairman of the Federal Reserve Board uttering the words, 'consumer protection.' It had not happened since 198 1."[66]

Currently, the staffing, the budgets, the expertise and the primary responsibilities of the Fed necessarily reflect the critical functions it performs: setting monetary policy and controlling the money supply, consolidated supervision of bank holding companies and the financial institutions those holding companies own to assure the safety and soundness of those groups, supervision of state-chartered member-banks in coordination with state regulators, and oversight of the federal reserve banks. Under this option the Fed would be required to accept consumer protection as a responsibility that is the equal of its other responsibilities, staff and budget for that function and, makes its operations in the area transparent. These responsibilities should be subject to specific oversight by a designated Board member.

Wherever it is placed, the success of the new regulator would depend in part on a statutory outline of the manner in which it would be related to the various financial institution regulatory agencies, and how those agencies would relate to one another, in dealing with consumer credit products. The agencies that are responsible for assuring the safety and soundness of the financial institutions would be able to pursue those goals without interference.

The point of the single regulatory authority would be only to assure that both financial institutions and non-financial institutions that issue consumer credit products must play on a level field, all meeting the minimum standards established by the federal agency. No one issuer could gain advantage by moving to a different regulator.

5. Create Executive Pay Structures That Discourage Excessive Risk Taking

Problem with current system: **Executive pay packages incentivize excessive risk.**

Executive pay is a key issue in modernizing the financial regulatory system. However, the common focus on the themes of inequality and "pay for performance" misses the unnecessary risk that many compensation schemes introduce into the financial sector. Altering the incentives that encourage this risk through the tax code, regulation, and corporate governance reform will help mitigate systemic risk in future crises.

Executive compensation has been one of the most controversial issues in American business since the late 1980s. In response to criticism that executives' and shareholders' interests did not sufficiently align,[67] executive compensation packages began to contain more and more stock options, to the point where options now represent the lion's share of a high-ranking executive's pay.[68]

Much criticism of executive pay has had its origins in the increase in the ratio of the pay of public company executives to average worker pay, from 42:1 in 1982 to over 400:1 in the early years of this decade.[69] Recent executive pay scandals, such as those associated with the backdating of stock options, have centered on efforts by executives to disconnect pay from performance without informing investors.[70] Numerous accounts of executive pay in the context of the financial crisis of 2007–08 have focused on large severance packages, often described as once again disconnecting pay from performance.[71]

However, even before the current crises, many criticized such incentive plans for encouraging excessive focus on the short term at the expense of consideration of the risks involved.[72] This short- term focus led to unsustainable stock buyback programs, accounting manipulations, risky trading and investment strategies, or other unsustainable business practices that merely yield short-term positive financial reports.

Executive pay should be designed, regulated, and taxed to incentivize financial executives to prioritize long-term objectives, and to avoid both undertaking excessive, unnecessary risk and socializing losses with the help of the federal taxpayer.

Action item: **Create tax incentives to encourage long-term–oriented pay packages.**

Financial firm packages typically have a number of features that introduce short-term biases in business decision making. Most equity-linked compensation is either in the form of performance bonuses, typically awarded on an annual basis, and options on restricted stock, typically awarded in the form of grants with three-year vesting periods, and no restrictions on sale after vesting. These structures, together with the typical five-years-or-less tenure of public company CEOs, often lead to a focus on investment horizons of less than three years.[73]

Altering the tax treatment of executive compensation packages in the interests of encouraging stability, lessening risks, and orienting finance executives toward long-term goals represents a relatively simple step toward solving the incentive problem. Such a change could result from revising applicable tax rates, changing the treatment of compensation as income versus capital gains, or other relatively simple measures.

Action item: **Encourage financial regulators to guard against asymmetric pay packages in financial institutions, such as options combined with large severance packages.**

Asymmetric links between compensation and risk create incentives for executives to pursue potentially systemically threatening high-risk–high-reward strategies without sufficient regard for the downside potential. Encouraging regulators to spot and discourage compensation packages that excessively insulate executives from losses will help resolve this asymmetry and promote stability.

Stock options create incentives that are tied to stock price, but the overall compensation package's asymmetric link to stock price actually helps encourage more dramatic risk taking. As the price of the underlying stock declines, the option holder become less sensitive to further declines in value of the underlying stock, and more interested in the possibility of achieving dramatic gains, regardless of the risk of further losses.[74]

A number of common features of executive pay practice that further protect executives against downside risk exacerbate this asymmetry problem.

Among these features are the prevalence of option repricing when the underlying company stock falls below the option strike price for sustained periods of time and large severance packages paid to failed executives.

While asymmetries in executive compensation are potentially harmful in the context of any company, they create particular difficulties in the context of regulated financial institutions. Most regulated financial institutions are the beneficiaries of explicit or implicit guarantees. The FDIC insurance system is an explicit guarantee to some depositors, which in the current crisis has been extended to all bank debt. The current Treasury and Federal Reserve rescues of Fannie Mae, Freddie Mac, and AIG, and the recent TARP actions in relation to Citigroup and Bank of America—and perhaps all nine major TARP recipient banks—all raise issues of implicit guarantees. These guarantees provide regulators with an opportunity to ensure that problematically asymmetrical compensation plans do not reappear in these institutions.

Action item: **Regulators should consider requiring executive pay contracts to provide for clawbacks of bonus compensation for executives of failing institutions**

Financial system regulators should consider revoking bonus compensation for executives of failing institutions that require federal intervention. Whether the federal government promises to support the institution before a crisis develops, as with Fannie Mae and Freddie Mac, or after, as with TARP recipients, the prospect of losing bonus compensation could deter risky practices that make the federal rescue more probable.

The cases of the Fannie Mae and Freddie Mac seem particularly relevant. In both companies, executive pay in the course of the 1990s moved from a model focused on corporate stability to a model focused on stock price maximization through asymmetric, short-term incentives. [75] It appears that this change fed pressures to increase margins in ways that were only possible by engaging in riskier investment practices. [76] This approach to executive pay is inconsistent with federal guarantees of solvency; inevitably, if it is not abandoned, taxpayers will end up paying for imprudent risk taking by improperly incentivized executives.

As the financial crisis has developed, there has been a fair amount of discussion of clawbacks of executive pay. The Sarbanes-Oxley Act of 2002 required clawbacks of executive pay awarded as a result of fraudulent financial statements.[77] Similar clawback provisions could help restore symmetry and a longer-term perspective to executive compensation systems. As such, regulators should consider adding them to the tools at their disposal.

***Action item:* Encourage corporate governance structures with stronger board and long-term investor oversight of pay packages**

The Associated Press recently reported that "even where banks cut back on pay, some executives were left with seven- or eight-figure compensation that most people can only dream about. Richard D. Fairbank, the chairman of Capital One Financial Corp., took a $1 million hit in compensation after his company had a disappointing year, but still got $17 million in stock options. The McLean, Va.-based company received $3.56 billion in bailout money on Nov. 14."[78]

Corporate governance regulations should strengthen the role of boards and long-term shareholders in the executive pay process with the goal of encouraging executive pay practices that align executives' interests with the long-term performance of the businesses they manage

The twin problems of asymmetric and short-term-focused executive pay have been the subject of a number of reform efforts by business groups. Such reform recommendations have come from the Conference Board, in its report on the origins of the financial crisis,[79] and from the Aspen Institute's Principles for Long Term Value Creation,[80] endorsed by the U.S. Chamber of Commerce and the Business Roundtable, as well as by the Council of Institutional Investors and the AFL-CIO.

Financial regulators should encourage these efforts wherever possible and provide assistance wherever practicable.

6. Reform the Credit Rating System

***Problem with current system:* The credit rating system is ineffective and plagued with conflicts of interest**

The major credit rating agencies played an important—and perhaps decisive—role in enabling (and validating) much of the behavior and decision making that now appears to have put the broader financial system at risk. In the subprime-related market specifically, high ratings for structured financial products—especially mortgage-backed securities (MBS), collateralized debt obligations (CDO), and CDOs that invested in other CDOs (frequently referred to as CDO-squared, or CDO^2)—were essential for ensuring broad demand for these products. High ratings not only instilled confidence in potentially risk-averse investors, but also helped satisfy investors' regulatory requirements, which were often explicitly linked to ratings from the major credit rating agencies. By 2006, Moody's business in rating structured financial products accounted for 44 percent of its revenues, as compared to 32 percent from its traditional corporate-bond rating business.[81] It has also been reported that "roughly 60 percent of all global structured products were AAA-rated, in contrast to less than 1 percent of corporate issues."[82] Financial firms, from Fannie Mae to AIG, also benefited greatly from having high credit ratings of their own—especially AAA—allowing them not only to borrow at low rates on the short-term markets to finance longer-term (and higher yielding) investments but also to sell guaranties of various sorts, effectively "renting out" their credit rating.

Numerous explanations have been offered for credit rating agencies' apparent mistakes, including conflicts of interest, misuse of complex models, and their quasi-public status as nationally recognized statistical rating organizations (NRSROs).

Regarding conflicts of interests, worrisome is the rating agencies' practice of charging issuers for their ratings, a practice that began at Fitch and Moody's in 1970 and at Standard & Poor's a few years later. [83] Although the practice of collecting payments from issuers has long provoked criticism, market observers often downplayed these concerns, suggesting that "the agencies have an overriding incentive to maintain a reputation for high-quality, accurate ratings."[84] Others, however, claim that the "issuer pays" model biases ratings upward and also encourages "ratings shopping" by issuers, which in turn provokes a race to the bottom on the part of the rating agencies, each willing to lower quality standards to drum up more business.[85]

Beyond the ratings themselves, credit rating agencies also charge issuers for advice, including pre- rating assessments (in which issuers learn what ratings will likely be under various hypothetical scenarios) and risk-management consulting. In some cases, credit rating agency analysts subsequently go to work for the companies they had been rating.[86] This revolving-door practice creates not only the potential for conflicts of interest but also for gaming of the system, since former employees of the rating agencies presumably know how best to exploit weaknesses in the agencies' risk assessment models.

Many critics charge that it was the models themselves—and overreliance on them—that got the credit rating agencies into trouble in recent years, particularly in assigning ratings to structured financial products. "Instead of focusing on actual diligence of the risks involved, demanding additional issuer disclosures, or scrutinizing collateral appraisers' assessments," writes one skeptic, "rating agencies primarily relied on mathematical models that estimated the loss distribution and simulated the cash flows of RMBS [residential mortgage backed securities] and CDOs using historical data." [87]

Many of the models involved excessively rosy assumptions about the quality of the underlying mortgages, ignoring the fact that these mortgages (especially subprime mortgages) were far riskier than ever before and were in fact becoming steadily riskier year by year. [88] Credit rating agency modeling of mortgage-related securities may also have involved mistaken assumptions about the independence of the underlying mortgages—including the assumption that defaults would not be highly correlated across a broad bundle of mortgages or mortgage-related securities.[89] By extension, many of the rating agencies' models may also have involved overly optimistic assumptions about the direction of housing prices (that is, that they would not fall by much, if at all). When asked on a conference call in March 2007 about how a 1 to 2 percent decline in home prices over an extended period of time would affect Fitch's modeling of certain subprime-related securities, a Fitch representative conceded, "The models would break down completely."[90]

Yet another problem plaguing the rating agencies' models was the practice of embedded structuring by issuers, according to which CDOs would themselves become inputs into new CDOs (CDO^2). "With multiple rounds of structuring," three finance professors explain, "even minute errors at the level of the underlying securities, which would be insufficient to alter the security's rating, can dramatically alter the ratings of the structured finance securities."[91]

Of particular concern from a regulatory standpoint is the extent to which state and federal (and even global) financial regulations are linked to private credit ratings—and, in fact, to ratings issued by just a handful of specially designated credit rating agencies, the NRSROs). To the extent that leading credit rating agencies enjoy a protected status and virtually guaranteed demand as a result of their regulatory significance, they may face diminished incentives to maintain the quality of their ratings.

The SEC has recently undertaken a number of reforms aimed at the operations of the NRSROs pursuant to the passage of the Credit Rating Agency Reform Act of 2006 (the Rating Agency Act), 92 which granted the SEC authority to implement registration, recordkeeping, financial reporting, and oversight rules with respect to registered credit rating agencies. Before this grant of authority to the SEC, NRSROs were essentially unregulated. Pursuant to its new regulatory authority, the SEC has registered ten firms;[93] instituted examinations of NRSROs' practices;[94] and proposed rules designed to enhance accountability, transparency, and competition.[95] The Rating Agency Act and the SEC's recent regulatory activity are positive developments. However, since 2006 the financial crisis has revealed the extent of the harmful consequences of the deep-seated conflicts of interest and distorted incentives associated with the credit ratings firms. With the knowledge that the contours of reform of credit rating agency regulation must take into account the SEC's actions, we propose the following recommendations.

Action item: **Adopt one or more regulatory options to address conflicts of interest and incentives.**

To address conflicts of interest, the SEC or a new regulatory body (see below) could impose limits on the proportion of revenues of rating agencies that are derived from issuers, though there is disagreement about whether alternative revenue sources would prove sufficient.[96] Alternatively, for each rating, issuers could be required to pay into a pool, from which a rating agency wouldbe chosen at random.[97] Here, the challenge would be to maintain the quality of ratings after severing the link between pay and performance. One could also imagine the introduction of grace periods in which credit rating analysts could not take jobs with their clients. While this too would limit conflicts of interest, it might also interfere with the recruiting of high-quality credit analysts at the rating agencies.

To improve incentives, the SEC or some other regulatory body should further encourage additional competition by progressively expanding the ranks of the NRSROs.[98] Other options would include additional disclosure requirements or prohibitions on rating agencies' use of nonpublic information.[99] Since rating agencies currently face little if any legal liability for malfeasance in the production of ratings, a number of experts have proposed strategies for imposing liability on credit rating agencies to ensure appropriate accountability.[100] Although such reforms might well prove helpful, they would be unlikely to solve the underlying problem by themselves.

Action item: **Reform the quasi-public role of NRSRO's and consider creating a Credit Rating Review Board.**

Perhaps the most pressing issue of all from a regulatory standpoint is the NRSRO designation itself. Particularly given all of the concerns that have been raised about the credit rating agencies and their poor performance leading up to the current crisis, state and federal policymakers will need to reassess whether they can continue to rely on these private ratings as a pillar of public financial regulation.[101] In fact, it may be time to consider the possibility of eliminating, or at least dramatically scaling back, the NRSRO designation and replacing it with something else.[102]

One option would be to create a public entity—a Credit Rating Review Board—that would have to sign off on any rating before it took on regulatory significance. Even if an asset was rated as investment grade by a credit rating agency, it could still not be added to a bank or pension fund portfolio, for example, unless the rating was also approved by the review board. Ideally, the board would be given direction by lawmakers to favor simpler (plain vanilla) instruments with relatively long track records. New and untested instruments might not make the cut. Of course, such new instruments could still be actively bought and sold in the private marketplace. Only regulated transactions that currently require ratings would be effected. Two key advantages of this approach are that it would permit a dramatic opening of the market for private credit ratings and at the same time discontinue the unsuccessful outsourcing of vital regulatory monitoring.

Another, substantially different, option for the design of such a Credit Rating Review Board would be to model the board in part on the Public Company Accounting Oversight Board (PCAOB), a nont-for-profit corporation that was created by the Sarbanes-Oxley Act to oversee the auditors of public companies.[103] Under this model, the Credit Rating Review Board would not rate instruments ex ante, but instead audit ratings after the fact, perhaps on an annual basis, to ensure that rating agencies are sufficiently disclosing their rating methodologies, the ratings agencies' methodologies are sound, and the rating agencies are adhering to their methodologies. Depending on the course of the SEC's rulemaking, the Credit Rating Review Board could coordinate with or assume some of the SEC's authority to regulate conflicts of interest and inspect, investigate, and discipline NRSROs.

7. Make Establishing a Global Financial Regulatory Floor a U.S. Diplomatic Priority

***Problem with current system:* The globalization of financial markets encourages countries to compete to attract foreign capital by offering increasingly permissive regulatory laws that increase market risk**

The rapid globalization of financial markets in recent decades has created a new set of problems for national regulators and exposed market participants to an additional element of risk. Capital is able to flow freely across international borders, while regulatory controls are bound to domestic jurisdictions. Private actors, therefore, have the benefit of seeking out regulatory climates that best accommodate their financial objectives.

Countries, in turn, bid for capital flows by adjusting their tax and regulatory schemes, as well as their legal infrastructure and employment laws. While New York and London tout their preeminence as financial capitals, Tokyo, Hong Kong, Singapore, Bahrain, and Doha, Qatar have all become financial hubs. At the same time, certain offshore tax havens, such as the Cayman Islands, the Bahamas, and the Channel Islands have developed local industries catering to the financial services needs of foreigners. Often, the sole comparative advantage offered by these locations is the opportunity to profit from "regulatory arbitrage." The consequence is a global race to the bottom whereby deregulation is pursued to the detriment of market stability.

Meanwhile, global markets have become increasingly interconnected. From 1990 to 2000, the total dollar amount of crossborder securities holdings where non-U.S. investors held U.S. securities, or vice versa, grew from approximately $1.5 trillion to approximately $6.9 trillion.[104] Today, U.S. issuers raise debt and equity funding in local markets all over the world. Conversely, foreign issuers who previously looked to the liquidity of the United States capital markets now find equally liquid pools of capital in Europe and Asia.

When financial turmoil strikes issuers or borrowers in one country, it is equally likely to have adverse consequences beyond national borders. The subprime mortgage crisis of 2008 caused widespread havoc outside the United States, beginning with a small thrift in England and sweeping over the world. At the same time the United States government initiated its $700 billion bailout plan, the United Kingdom established a facility to make additional capital available to eight of its largest banks and building societies, the governments of France, Belgium, Luxembourg and the Netherlands made large capital infusions to bail out major banks operating in those countries, and the government of Iceland was forced to take over the three largest banks there. 105 Stock markets worldwide plunged. Investors large and small suffered.

The abiding lesson is that booms and busts can no longer be restricted to their country of origin. Nations must embark on aggressive diplomatic efforts to address the collective risks posed by today's globalized financial markets.

***Action item:* Build alliances with foreign partners to create a global financial regulatory floor.**

Given the ease with which money moves across international borders, it is difficult for one country to adopt a system to provide adequate regulation of the capital markets, as well as adequate consumer protection, unless all major participants in the global economy have agreed to coordinated action beforehand. Otherwise, regulatory arbitrage and the resulting race to the bottom are inevitable. To assure the stability of the markets, it is therefore imperative for U.S. financial market regulators, as well as the State Department, to work together to encourage greater harmonization of regulatory standards, as well as broad adoption of a floor of recognized "prudent regulatory measures."

Better coordination of regulation and surveillance, while difficult to achieve, will result in better- regulated entities that are less likely to cause damages to global markets and other market participants. It is also likely to result in more efficient and less costly regulation for regulated entities.

***Action item:* Actively participate in international organizations that are designed to strengthen communication and cooperation among national regulators.**

Financial services regulators have created a number of organizations to share ideas and information regarding financial services entities and markets. These include the Basel Committee on Bank Supervision (BCBS), the Senior Supervisors Group (SSG), and the International Organization of Securities Commissions (IOSCO). The SSG, for one, meets regularly to discuss supervisory matters and to issue recommendations for better supervision.[106]

The SSG also periodically sponsor "colleges of supervisors," in which supervisors from several countries that have jurisdiction over part of the operations of a globally active financial services firm will convene to discuss issues regarding regulation of the firm. Established linkages between regulators with different perspectives on a particular entity facilitate information-sharing that enables all supervisors to better understand the risks facing the entity. These relationships also ensure better coordination during times of stress. These efforts should be expanded to include consideration of systemically important financial institutions, in order to develop a better understanding of the risk profiles of such institutions and to improve their ability to intervene where the risk profile increases to potentially destabilizing levels.

8. Plan for the Next Crisis

***Problem with current system:* Participants, observers, and regulators neither predicted nor developed contingency plans to address the current crisis**

Despite calls for caution from some quarters, very few observers predicted the severity of the current collapse in the housing, debt, and equity markets, or the massive decline in economic activity. Those commentators who most vocally raised doubts about the sustainability of housing prices, the pace of derivatives growth, or lax regulation were largely dismissed as fearmongers, or as simply "not getting it."[107]

Traditional measures of financial and economic exposure, such as bank capitalization, troubled loans, stock prices, and money supply growth, indicated only moderate exposure to a sharp asset price collapse and a severe recession.[108] Yet there was a compelling case for concern based on a closer examination of the multiple layers of leverage invested in housing assets and their derivatives.[109] More broadly, stagnant household productivity, the pace of financial product innovation and the increased leverage on Wall Street might all have set off alarm bells.[110]

Indeed, some analysts see systemic collapses as inherently more likely in complex, interdependent systems such as our modern financial environment.[111] While most destructive outcomes are deemed to be so unlikely, based on historical comparisons, that they are not worth considering, recent analysis indicates on the contrary that complex systems produce these "outlier" results on a counterintuitively regular basis.[112]

Current institutions are not likely to fare better in the future. Governments, industry, Wall Street, and academia typically employ economists with similar training and backgrounds to create their forecasts, leading to procyclical optimism and convergence of economic forecasts. In particular, economists have a truly dismal record in predicting the onset of recessions and asset crashes.[113] Given the risk of a similar collapse in the future and the lack of formal processes in business or government requiring that the truly dismal scenarios be assessed, the current system will likely face similar risks not long after the present crisis is resolved.

***Action item:* Create Financial Risk Council of outside experts to report to Congress and regulators on possible looming challenges**

To promote better planning, financial experts should be aiming to identify the problems of the future, much as the military does. To this end, the Panel recommends establishing a Financial Risk Council featuring a truly diverse group of opinions, a formal mechanism whereby the concerns, both individual and collective, of this group will be regularly brought to the attention of Congress and financial regulators, with a focus on precisely those low-likelihood, huge-magnitude developments that consensus opinion will dismiss.

The council should consider all potential domestic and foreign threats to the stability of the U.S. financial systems. These sources of threat should include, but not be limited to: (1) economic shocks and recessions; (2) asset booms and busts; (3) fiscal, trade, foreign exchange, and monetary imbalances; (4) infrastructure failures, natural disaster, and epidemics; (5) institutional mismanagement; (6) crime, fraud; and terrorism; (7) legislative and regulatory failure; and (8) failed product and process innovation.

Strong, independent thinking among the membership of the Council will be critical: every effort should be made to avoid an optimistic consensus that there are no major threats looming. To that end, Council members should represent a diverse array of stakeholders, with a record of speaking their minds.

The council would be required to publish regular reports to Congress and to select among various techniques for identifying threats. These approaches might include:

1. **Wargaming:** Teams represent various market, government, regulatory, and subversive constituents. A control team sets up the initial environment and introduces destabilizing changes. The teams respond in real time and the control group feeds the impacts of their decisions into the environment. Subsequent to the wargame, there is an examination of outcomes, the level of constituent preparedness, and the quality of the risk management processes.

2. **Strategic scenario analysis:** An analytic team works backward from worst-case financial crisis outcomes to identify the potential triggering factors and preventative or mitigating solutions. This approach prevents the "it couldn't happen" mindset.

3. **Nonlinear modeling/"black swan" sensitivity analysis:** An analytic team assumes previously unseen levels for key variables in order to destabilize financial models and observes break points and systemic failures.

A Financial Risk Council composed of strong, divergent voices should avoid overly optimistic consensus and conventional wisdom, keeping Congress appropriately concerned and energized about known and unknown risks in a complex, highly interactive environment.

V. ISSUES REQUIRING FURTHER STUDY

There are several important questions regarding financial regulatory reform that are beyond the scope of this Report, and will require further attention.

First, the Panel has identified three highly technical issues relating to the financial regulatory system, and recommends that the relevant regulatory agencies take up specialized review of these questions. These are:

1. *Accounting rules*: Further study is required to identify needed reforms of the current accounting rules, particularly with connection to systemic risk. Among the issues that should be considered are mark-to-market accounting, mark-to-model accounting, fair-value accounting, issues of procyclicality, accounting for contingent liabilities, and off-balancesheet items.

2. *Securitization*: Further study is required to consider the logic and limits of securitization, and reform options such as requiring issuers to retain a portion of offering, phased compensation based on loan or pool performance, and other requirements.

3. *Short-selling*: In light of recent imposed limits, regulation of short-selling should be further studied and long-term policies should be developed.

Second, the Panel plans to address regulatory architecture more thoroughly in a subsequent report, including the issues of co-regulation, universal banking, regulatory capture, the revolving door problem, bankruptcy and receivership issues involving financial institutions, and the division of regulatory responsibilities.

VI. ACKNOWLEDGMENTS

The Panel owes a debt of gratitude to many people who helped produce this report. Our deepest thanks go to Professor David Moss of Harvard Business School, who played a key role in conceptualizing and drafting the report. He was ably assisted by Melanie Wachtell, who worked long hours both to direct the underlying research efforts and to help pull the final draft together. The Panel is also grateful to Christopher Caines for his meticulous and thoughtful editing of this report. We express our thanks to Professor Arthur Wilmarth, Professor Patricia McCoy, Professor Ronald Mann, Professor Julio Rotemberg, Professor David Scharfstein, and Dr. Robert Litan, all of whom read portions of the draft and made helpful comments. Ganesh Sitaraman and Jonathan Lackow offered important drafting assistance. Thanks are also due to Abbye Atkinson, Brett Arnold, Cole Bolton, Marc Farris, Arthur Kimball-Stanley, Gregory Lablanc, Eric Nguyen, Adam Pollet, Walter Rahmey, Chris Theodoridis, Patrick Tierney, and Chieh-Ting Yeh, who contributed careful and detailed research to this undertaking.

The Panel also gratefully acknowledges the assistance of Christine Sgarlata Chung, assistant clinical professor of law and director of the Securities Arbitration Clinic at Albany Law School, and David P. McCaffrey, distinguished teaching professor at Albany–SUNY, the co-directors of the Center for Financial Market Regulation, in preparing the summaries of prior reports on regulatory reform contained in the appendix and the longer summaries of those reports that may be found on the Panel's Web site, cop.senate.

The Panel is also grateful to the following individuals who generously provided their time and expertise to the preparation of this report: Tobias Adrian, Professor Edward Balleisen, Dean Baker, Brandon Becker, Pervenche Beres, Professor Bruce Carruthers, Professor Lord Eatwell, Douglas Engmann, former Senator Phil Gramm, Professor Michael Greenberger, Professor Joseph Grundfest, Michael Jamroz, Robert Kelly, Professor Naomi Lamoreaux, Professor Stan Liebowitz, Professor Andrew Lo, David Raboy, Professor Hal Scott, L.W. Seidman, Professor Jay Westbrook, Professor Luigi Zingales, Professor Todd Zywicki, and the Squam Lake Working Group on Financial Regulation (including Martin Baily, Andrew Bernard, John Campbell, John Cochrane, Doug Diamond, Darrell Duffie, Ken French, Anil Kashyap, Rick Mishkin, Raghu Rajan, David Scharfstein, Matt Slaughter, Bob Shiller, Hyun Song Shin, Jeremy Stein, and Rene Stulz). The Panel thanks the following institutions and organizations for their contributions: Business Roundtable (including John Castellani and Tom Lehner), the Chicago Board Options Exchange, the Financial Industry Regulatory Authority, the Council of Institutional Investors (including Anne Yerger, Amy Borrus, and Jeff Mahoney), the Consumer Federation of America (and Barbara Roper), the International Swaps and Derivatives Association (and Robert Pickel), and the National Consumer Law Center (including Lauren Saunders and Margot Saunders). The Panel also benefited from the guidance of David Einhorn, Sarah Kelsey, Arthur Levitt, Alex Pollock, Professor Robert Merton, and Lawrence Uhlick.

VII. About the Congressional Oversight Panel

In response to the escalating crisis, on October 3, 2008, Congress provided the U.S. Department of the Treasury with the authority to spend $700 billion to stabilize the U.S. economy, preserve home ownership, and promote economic growth. Congress created the Office of Financial Stabilization (OFS) within Treasury to implement a Troubled Asset Relief Program (TARP). At the same time, Congress created the Congressional Oversight Panel to "review the current state of financial markets and the regulatory system." The Panel is empowered to hold hearings, review official data, and write reports on actions taken by Treasury and financial institutions and their effect on the economy. Through regular reports, the Panel must oversee Treasury's actions, assess the impact of spending to stabilize the economy, evaluate market transparency, ensure effective foreclosure mitigation efforts, and guarantee that Treasury's actions are in the best interests of the American people. In addition, Congress has instructed the Panel to produce a special report on regulatory reform that will analyze "the current state of the regulatory system and its effectiveness at overseeing the participants in the financial system and protecting consumers."

On November 14, 2008, Senate Majority Leader Harry Reid and the Speaker of the House Nancy Pelosi appointed Richard H. Neiman, Superintendent of Banks for the State of New York, Damon Silvers, Associate General Counsel of the American Federation of Labor and Congress of Industrial Organizations (AFL-CIO), and Elizabeth Warren, Leo Gottlieb Professor of Law at Harvard Law School to the Panel. With the appointment on November 19 of Congressman Jeb Hensarling to the Panel by House Minority Leader John Boehner, the Panel had a quorum and met for the first time on November 26, 2008, electing Professor Warren as its chair. On December 16, 2008, Senate Minority Leader Mitch McConnell named Senator John E. Sununu to the Panel, completing the Panel's membership.

Congressman Hensarling and former Senator Sununu did not approve this report. Their alternative view is included in the following section.

VIII. Additional Views

Richard H. Neiman

I am pleased to support the Panel's special report on regulatory reform, which begins to address some of the most critical issues facing our nation, such as improving consumer protection, reducing systemic risk, eliminating regulatory gaps, and enhancing global co-ordination of supervision.

These are precisely the issues we need to address in these unprecedented times, when Americans are losing their homes, and the financial system and our economy are at greater risk than at any time since the Depression.

Addressing any one of these issues individually would be a challenge; compiling a report that addresses them all within nine short weeks was a herculean task. Given the diversity of backgrounds and ideological views of the panel members, the fact that we have reached agreement on the critical issues and on many action items to address those issues is truly remarkable.

As the only regulator on the panel, I find it appropriate to highlight certain issues of particular importance and to which I bring a unique perspective.

- States must be allowed to increase their role in protecting consumers

States have long strived to protect their citizens from harmful financial products and should continue to carry out this vital role. States, like New York, sounded an early alarm on subprime lending by adopting anti-predatory lending legislation and reaching landmark settlements with the nation's top mortgage bankers, providing hundreds of millions of dollars in consumer restitution and improving industry practices.

Rather than join with the states, however, the OCC and the OTS thwarted state efforts, by claiming broad field preemption and then failing to adopt measures that protected consumers. This federal overreach caused gaps in consumer protection standards, as more protective state laws were set aside without being replaced by appropriate national standards or equivalent enforcement efforts.

I want to underscore the Panel's recommendation to eliminate federal preemption of state consumer laws and confirm the ability of states to examine and enforce compliance with federal and state consumer protection laws. The recommendations will restore the appropriate balance between federal and state regulators and provide the basis for a "New Federalism." It will draw on what is best about our current dual banking system, close gaps in consumer protection, and maximize the effectiveness of the joint resources of state and federal regulators.

- THE FEDERAL RESERVE BOARD SHOULD SET MINIMUM FEDERAL STANDARDS FOR CONSUMER PROTECTION

The Panel's report calls for the establishment of a single federal regulator that would have overarching consumer protection responsibilities, such as setting national minimum standards. We need to establish adequate baseline consumer protections for all Americans. Under this proposal, states could adopt more stringent requirements than the federal body, as local conditions warranted, and could regulate consumer protection standards in the absence of federal action. This would allow states to serve as incubators to develop innovative regulatory solutions. Laws that are tried first at the state level and found successful often serve as the model for laws at the national level.

The national minimum standards should go beyond required disclosures and extend to substantive regulation of consumer financial products. Disclosure alone does not address the issues that gave rise to the current crisis. We need to address key issues, including affordability, suitability, and the duty of care owed by financial services providers to consumers.

While I wholeheartedly support a heightened emphasis on consumer issues, I believe the functions of consumer protection should not be separated from the role of safety and soundness. Loans that take unfair advantage of consumers adversely affect the safety and soundness of financial institutions. Regulators must consider an institution's activities holistically, to detect emerging problems and have adequate tools to respond. Too narrow a mission could lead to myopic, impractical regulations, increasing the likelihood of negative unintended consequences and threatening to undermine the safety and soundness of financial institutions. Assigning the consumer protection function to a new stand-alone agency with a limited mandate would create yet another federal bureaucracy, at a time when I believe we need to be streamlining and avoiding counterproductive regulatory turf wars.

I recognize that the Federal Reserve Board may have been slow to take up consumer protection responsibilities placed on it by Congress. However, I believe that the current crisis has demonstrated to the Fed the importance of consumer protection to the health of our financial institutions and the economy as a whole.

- THE FEDERAL RESERVE BOARD SHOULD BE THE SYSTEMIC REGULATOR

The Panel's report correctly identifies the need for a federal systemic risk regulator, and I concur with proposals, such as those by the Group of Thirty, that this role be performed by a country's central bank.

The current crisis has demonstrated that the Federal Reserve Board, our nation's central bank, is ideally suited to harness the tools available to it to address systemic risk. The Fed has played a pivotal role in designing and implementing solutions to the current financial crisis and has gained unparalleled insight into risks presented by non-banking as well as banking institutions. However, the Fed still has no explicit authority over many non-banking organizations that meet the definition for being "systemically significant." The Fed's function in setting monetary policy, as well as supervising banking organizations and providing discount window facilities, strategically places it at the heart of the nation's regulatory nerve center. Creating new agencies to perform these broader systemic tasks would needlessly duplicate existing functions, dilute current levels of expertise and fail to take advantage of the wealth of experience accumulated by the Fed. The Federal Reserve's mission could easily be updated to formally incorporate these tasks into a broader mandate. I am confident that result would be a healthier, more vibrant financial system.

- WE NEED TO RESTORE THE CONFIDENCE OF THE AMERICAN PUBLIC

As the Panel's report states, we need to restore a proper balance between free markets and the regulatory framework, in order to ensure that those markets operate to protect the economy, honest market participants and the public. I look forward to working with Congress to address the issues the report identifies, so that we can restore the confidence of the American public in the financial services system.

Congressman Jeb Hensarling and Former Senator John E. Sununu

Preface

As part of the Economic Emergency Stabilization Act of 2008 (Pub. L. No. 110-343), Congress required that the newly established Congressional Oversight Panel (the Panel) prepare a report "analyzing the current state of the regulatory system and its effectiveness at overseeing the participants in the financial system and protecting consumers, and providing recommendations for improvement, including recommendations regarding whether any participants in the financial markets that are currently outside the regulatory system should become subject to the regulatory system, the rationale underlying such recommendation, and whether there are any gaps in existing consumer protections." Even in an environment where dozens of organizations have already offered their own perspective on the economic crisis and regulatory reform, assembling such a document in the short time the Panel has been in operation would be a daunting task. Adding to the challenge, the Panel is a diverse group which possessed a dedicated, but minimal staff well into the middle of January. As a result, much of the work drafting the Panel Report was given to individuals outside its operation.

Building consensus over such a broad range of economic questions would be difficult in any event. The timing and process for preparing this document, unfortunately, made it more so. Given the differences that remain regarding our views of the systemic weaknesses that led to the crisis, and, more important, policy recommendations for reform, we have chosen not to support the Panel Report as presented. Instead, we provide here a more concise statement of the underlying causes of the current financial crisis and a series of recommendations for regulatory modernization. While there are several points in the Panel Report with which we agree, we also provide a summary of several areas where our disagreement led us to oppose the final product.

This statement is organized into several sections:

1. Introduction
2. Observations on Current State of Financial Regulation
3. Underlying Causes of the Credit Crisis
4. Recommendations for Financial Service Regulatory Modernization and Reform
5. Differences with Congressional Oversight Panel Recommendations

In preparing this summary, we drew heavily from several sources, which presented a range of views, but in which we also shared many common themes and recommendations. These include the Group of 30's *Financial Reform: A Framework for Financial Stability*, the Committee on Capital Markets Regulation's *Recommendations for Reorganizing the U.S. Financial Regulatory Structure*, the GAO's *A Framework for Crafting and Assessing Proposals to Modernize the Outdated U.S. Financial Regulatory System*, and the Department of the Treasury's *Blueprint for a Modernized Financial Regulatory Structure*. Others playing an influential role in helping frame the often complicated policy questions engendered by this work include the scholars at the American Enterprise Institute (AEI), particularly Peter Wallison and Alex Pollock, as well as those at George Mason University's Mercatus Center, including Professor Todd Zywicki, Houman B. Shadab, and Satya Thallam.

If one theme emerged among others in these differing perspectives on the challenges ahead, it is that our pursuit should not be simply to identify new rules or areas in which to regulate, but to build a structure and system that is modern and appropriate to the institutions and technologies being used every day. A well-designed system should enhance market discipline, minimize risks to taxpayers, and avoid the pitfalls of unintended consequences. We hope our recommendations are true to these objectives.

Introduction

Since the collapse and rescue of Bear Stearns in March 2008, legislators, regulators, and financial market participants have found themselves enmeshed in a discussion of whether the financial system needs to be saved, and, if so, how best to save it. In October 2008, Congress passed the Emergency Economic Stabilization Act (EESA), which made available $700 billion for the purpose of purchasing mortgage-backed securities from financial institutions in hope of stabilizing the financial system. Shortly after Congress voted to make these funds available, the Treasury Department changed course and instead decided to purchase capital in the nation's financial institutions to free up credit markets.

Recent events—including additional losses by the nation's financial institutions, new Treasury programs to support two of the country's largest financial firms, and reports that the sums spent thus far on recapitalizing financial institutions have had only modest impact—demonstrate that while identifying problems in a marketplace might be easy, the task of isolating those problems, diagnosing their cause, and discerning how best to address them remains challenging. The conversation over how best to revive the financial system continues, and despite its urgency, it is essential that the participants in that conversation not rush to act in pursuit of a plan that fails to solve the problems we face, or makes them worse.

Beyond the pressing challenges to stabilize our economic system, however, is the broader question of how best to oversee our financial system. If reorganization is to be done responsibly, it will demand an extraordinary amount of study, research, thought, and discussion, beginning with a careful, unbiased consideration of what exactly led to the crisis that now threatens our financial system. The observations and recommendations contained in these views should therefore be viewed as a preliminary contribution to the debate, not the final word. If not for reasons of modesty, then for reasons of prudence and responsibility, readers should be cautioned that this represents the opening round of a longer conversation regarding the future of our financial system.

While the rapid escalation of the credit crisis last fall forced Congress to forgo a more deliberative process in considering policy options to respond, it is widely acknowledged now by both proponents and opponents of congressional action that properly addressing this crisis will involve a more carefully crafted response than the broadly defined powers given to Treasury under the $700 billion EESA. The stakes are no less important in regulating our financial system, for the consequences of mistakes made in rushing to fix a problem not fully understood will sow the seeds of even greater problems in the future.

As a precursor for constructive reform, policy makers must first avoid a reflexive urge to simply write new rules. In the wake of the largest financial crisis since the Great Depression, some have called immediately to “reregulate” the financial system to prevent calamities like this from occurring again. Those that believe that regulation is the only answer, however, ignore the significant ways in which government intervention magnified our existing problems. In fact, there are few, if any, segments of the economy in which government regulates, intervenes, and legislates as heavily as it does in the financial and housing sectors. Before embracing more government regulation as the only answer, such advocates should consider the many ways in which government regulation itself can be part of the problem. The history of financial regulation is replete with such examples as either regulators or regulation have simply failed or made matters worse.

In fact, the hallmark of past efforts to regulate the financial system has been that government regulation frequently fails. History has also repeatedly shown us that adding rigid new government regulations in the midst of a crisis to solve existing problems may be like the old military adage of armies being prepared to fight the last war. For example:

1. For decades, banking regulators tried to fix deposit prices nationally through "Regulation Q," which effectively denied savers significant amounts of interest and, in turn, imperiled thrifts and banks as deposits fled when interest rates were high. As with all government regulation, Reg Q was grounded in the belief that government mandates could manage market forces and keep banks safer.
2. Twenty years ago, in response to the failure of 1,600 commercial banks in the savings and loan crisis, the federal government enacted the Federal Deposit Insurance Corporation Improvement Act of 1991 (Pub..L. No. 102-242) (FDICIA), which significantly tightened bank and S&L regulation in an attempt to generate stability. However, the tougher restrictions of FDICIA did not fix the problem, and the savings and loan crisis ended up costing American taxpayers over $120 billion.[114]
3. More recently, state and federal legislation mandated the use of credit ratings from a few rating agencies, which effectively transformed these agencies into a government-sponsored cartel. What began as an impulse to bring safety and objectivity to the regulation of broker-dealers ended by creating a concentrated point of failure, jeopardizing the entire financial system.
4. Finally, there is the example of the Federal Reserve's effort to use monetary policy to avoid the recessionary effects of the tech bubble's bursting, only to find that in doing so, it had helped create the housing bubble.

In addition to its demonstrated failure in preventing financial collapse, regulation imposes significant costs on the financial system in several ways. For example, rather than increasing stability and enhancing safety, regulation can invite chaos and encourage otherwise irrational risk taking among market participants who falsely believe that government will act as a guardian angel to protect them. Market participants thus underprice risk because they conjecture government has managed the risks that market participants would otherwise have had to assess. However, in reality, any government—from our current one to the most heavy-handed of all totalitarian central planners—can never completely regulate a market given its resource constraints and the ingenuity of individual entrepreneurs with a proper profit motive.

Regulation can also reduce competition because its costs are more easily borne by large companies than by small ones. Large companies also have the ability to influence regulators to adopt regulations that favor their operations over those of smaller competitors. This is particularly true when regulations add costs that smaller companies cannot bear. Take, for example, the continuing decline in the number of community banks, the locally owned and operated institutions at the heart of many small towns and cities across the county. In 2004, the Federal Deposit Insurance Corporation (FDIC) released a report on the future of banking that found that although community banks still make up a majority of the banking industry, the number of community banks had been cut almost in half since 1985. The report also found that their deposit share has also declined significantly in that time frame as large banks extended their geographic reach.[115] Regulation also may keep low cost producers or international competitors out of regulated markets.

Regulation can also harm consumers in the form of higher costs, less innovation, and fewer choices. Regulatory costs are passed along to consumers through higher prices for services or products. For an example, one need only look at their monthly telephone bill to see firsthand how the cost of various government regulations imposed on phone services are directly passed onto consumers in the form of new fees. Since the application of regulations over a population is generally universal but the direct benefits are often only individually realized, many regulations end up imposing costs on all consumers for the benefit of a limited few. Additionally, the associated cost of some regulations end up exceeding their value by adding costs to the process of developing new products or new services. There are countless examples of this phenomenon in the insurance industry, where it can take years to achieve the regulatory approval needed to roll out a new product offering or, in some bewildering cases, to enact rate reductions for the benefit of consumers if the reduction is approved at all.[116]

Instead of creating new regulatory hurdles, a superior approach to better protect consumers and preserve wealth-creating opportunities is to enhance and reinforce wise regulation while bolstering private sector market discipline. This belief was well articulated in March 2000, when Gary Gensler, then Under Secretary for Domestic Finance in President Clinton's Treasury Department and currently President Obama's nominee to chair the Commodity Futures Trading Commission (CFTC), testified before the House Financial Services Committee regarding systemic risk in our capital markets. Over the course of his remarks, Gensler explained that instead of advocating for new or increased regulations, the approach supported by Treasury emphasized the formative role of the private sector in protecting market participants:

> The public sector has three roles.... Promoting market discipline means crafting government policy so that creditors do not rely on governmental intervention to safeguard them against loss.
>
> Transparency is the necessary corollary to market discipline. The government cannot impose market discipline, but it can enhance its effectiveness by promoting transparency. Transparency lessens uncertainty and thereby promotes market stability.
>
> Promoting competition in financial markets lessens systemic risk. The task of public policy must be to ensure the stability and integrity of the market system. In any sector of the financial market, the dominance of one or two firms can lessen competition and the efficiency of the market pricing mechanism. In addition, the entry of a subsidized financial institution into a market may motivate other firms to take on greater risks and weaken their operating results.[117]

Under Secretary Gensler had the right idea then, and his words should help provide the framework for the structural changes to our regulatory regime that we are now considering.

Observations on Current State of Financial Regulation

The United States has the most robust, accessible, and sound financial structure of any country in the world. That structure has provided unparalleled opportunities for millions, from seasoned market participants to casual investors to hardworking teachers and nurses hoping to live out the American dream. The success of our structure has been based on market discipline coupled with an appropriate level of regulation that fosters competition, transparency, and accountability.

Yet recently, this approach has been attacked by a small but vocal chorus claiming that two decades of financial deregulation has initiated the crisis that our financial system is now facing. These advocates of expanded government power contend that for years, government has been hard at work repealing all aspects of regulation in our financial sector. However, while such rhetoric might elicit some populist appeal, such claims do not bear scrutiny because the facts simply do not exist to support them.

One frequent argument heard from many critics is that the Gramm-Leach-Bliley Act (P.L. 106- 102), which repealed the Depression-era Glass-Steagall Act's separation of investment and commercial banking, was somehow responsible for the current credit crisis. To the contrary, a wide variety of experts across the political spectrum have dismissed that claim as "a handy scapegoat"[118] at best. When asked in October 2008 if Gramm-Leach-Bliley was a mistake, Alice M. Rivlin, the former director of both the Congressional Budget Office and the Office of Management and Budget, testified: "I don't think so, I don't think we can go back to a world in which we separate different kinds of financial services and say these lines cannot be crossed. That wasn't working very well.... We can't go back to those days, we have got to figure out how to go forward."[119] Even former President Bill Clinton remarked in a 2008 interview that "I don't see that signing that bill had anything to do with the current crisis."[120] If anything, Gramm-Leach-Bliley has played a significant role in attenuating the severity of this crisis by allowing commercial banks to merge with floundering investment banks—like JPMorgan Chase and Bear Stearns, Bank of America and Merrill Lynch, and Goldman Sachs and Morgan Stanley—actions that would have been explicitly prohibited had the Glass-Steagall Act still been in effect.

Although the advocates for expanded government power would have you believe otherwise, a careful examination of the historical record points toward the conclusion that regulation of the financial services sector has at least held constant if not substantially *increased* in recent years. One need only think about the sprawling regulatory mandate that the Sarbanes-Oxley Act (P.L. 107-204) imposed upon our financial system. Intended to toughen financial reporting requirements in the wake of the Enron scandal, Sarbanes-Oxley has created many needed reforms but its burden has also resulted in many companies taking their business—and their money—overseas. The result has been a flow of capital away from the U.S., capital which could have helped to shore-up American banks. In addition to Sarbanes-Oxley, over the last twenty years the federal government has implemented a wide array of new regulations on banks, mortgage lenders, and other financial services companies. These new regulations include:

1. The Federal Deposit Insurance Corporation Improvement Act of 1991 (P.L. 102-242), which was designed to improve bank supervision, examinations, and capital requirements.
2. The Home Ownership and Equity Protection Act (HOEPA) of 1994 (P.L. 103-325), which mandates enhanced disclosures by lenders who make certain high-cost refinancing loans to borrowers.
3. The 1989 and 2002 expansions of the mandated data furnished by lenders under the Home Mortgage Disclosure Act (HMDA).

4. The 2001 Bank Secrecy Act amendments made by the USA PATRIOT Act (P.L. 107-56), which enhanced anti-terrorist and money laundering record-keeping requirements for banks.
5. The Fair and Accurate Credit Transactions Act of 2003 (P.L. 108-159), which created new information sharing, indentify theft protection, and consumer disclosure mandates.
6. The Bankruptcy Abuse Prevention and Consumer Protection Act of 2005 (P.L. 109-8), which required lenders to provide new disclosures regarding credit offers and interest rates.
7. Various other Truth in Lending Act (TILA)/Regulation Z regulations and other federal banking agency guidance regarding lending, offers of credit, and consumer protections.

In fact, instead of wholesale deregulation, the case can be made that government has made concerted efforts to strengthen the very regulations that helped set the stage for the current financial crisis. To take one obvious example, there has been a strengthening of the Community Reinvestment Act, which has encouraged banks to make mortgage loans to borrowers who previously would have been rejected as non-creditworthy. Also, the Department of Housing and Urban Development's (HUD) affordable housing mandates for the government-sponsored enterprises (GSEs) were steadily increased from the 1990s through 2008, adding new targets and rules that compelled Fannie and Freddie to take certain loan purchasing actions to stay in compliance. Additionally, U.S. bank regulators are moving to quickly implement new capital requirements through the Basel II capital accord, which was less than two years old when plans for its adoption were announced on September 30, 2005. These untested rules will replace the Basel I rules that generally assigned lower capital charges for housing assets, which tended to increase the leveraging of housing-related assets, making our financial system less stable.[121]

Furthermore, proponents of the "regulation is the cure" argument must bear in mind that the most egregious financial failures have occurred not in the unregulated financial markets of hedge funds and over-the-counter derivatives, but in the highly regulated world of commercial and investment banking, where regulation has been the most burdensome. The former U.S. investment banks— which bought the so-called toxic assets that have been identified as one of the root causes of the financial crisis—were regulated by the Securities and Exchange Commission (SEC). Yet that supervision was insufficient to prevent the collapse of Bear Stearns or Lehman Brothers, two of this nation's largest investment banks, or the charter transformation of two other large investment banks, Goldman Sachs and Morgan Stanley, into bank holding companies. The credit rating agencies that blessed these products with AAA ratings were also regulated by the SEC, yet that supervision was not enough to prevent the inaccurate evaluations and gross errors in judgment of those agencies.

This nation's highly regulated commercial banks, subject to regulation by several agencies similarly snapped up large quantities of these assets, all while supposedly under the oversight and supervision of their regulators. Yet the results of this country's heavy regulation of commercial banks have also been abysmal. Wachovia, formerly the nation's fourth largest bank, was regulated by the Comptroller of the Currency (OCC). Countrywide Financial was a national bank under OCC supervision until mid-2007, and then it became a federal thrift regulated by the Office of Thrift Supervision (OTS). Washington Mutual, IndyMac and Downey Savings and Loan Association were all also federal thrifts regulated by the OTS. All five were well regulated. And the housing market collapse caused all five to fail.[122]

By contrast, many of the less stringently regulated actors in the financial system, such as hedge funds and other private pools of capital, and less stringently regulated products, such as derivatives and swaps traded over the counter, seem to have weathered the crisis better than their highly regulated counterparts. While investors in some of those products have lost money, and some of the companies engaged in those lines of business have closed their doors, these failures did not produce massive systemic risk concerns that required federal intervention placing taxpayer dollars at risk.

These observations lead to the clear point that heavy regulation, despite the outsized claims made for its effectiveness in avoiding crisis, will not solve our problems. As financial historian Bernard Shull stated in a 1993 paper on the matter:

> Comprehensive banking reform, traditionally including augmented and improved supervision, has typically evoked a transcendent, and in retrospect, unwarranted optimism. The Comptroller of the Currency announced in 1914 that, with the new Federal Reserve Act, "financial and commercial crises or panics ... Seem to be mathematically impossible." Seventy-five years later, confronting the S&L disaster with yet another comprehensive reform ... The Secretary of the Treasury proclaimed "two watchwords guided us as we undertook to solve this problem: Never Again."[123]

More than fifteen years after Shull's paper, many stand ready to march down the same well-worn path, clinging to the belief that heavy-handed regulation holds the answer. Those claims should be rejected. There is a better and more effective path to choose.

A brief history of the subprime crisis

To some observers, the turmoil in the U.S. financial markets, caused by severe dislocations in the country's housing markets, has heralded the end of the free-market system. But with all due respect to the critics of capitalism, the economic crisis in which the country now finds itself reflects not the failure of the free-market system, but more so the result of decades of misguided government policies that interfered with the functioning of that system. While recent events demonstrate a need for regulatory reform, modernization, and improvement, the larger lesson is that a number of well- meaning but clearly misguided government policies distorted America's housing markets, which in turn produced grave consequences for the financial system and the underlying economy.

In a rush to be seen as doing "something" in response, the advocates of expanded government power have brought forward a range of old proposals to regulate, reregulate, and overregulate any and every aspect of our economy. We believe a more practical approach would be to identify and correct the government policies that inflated the housing bubble underlying this crisis and then decide what change is necessary. Thus, the essential debate is not between deregulation and re- regulation, but instead between *wise* regulation and *counterproductive* regulation. Wise regulation helps make markets more competitive and transparent, empowers consumers with effective disclosure to make rational decisions, effectively polices markets for force and fraud, and reduces systemic risk. Counterproductive regulation hampers competitive markets, creates moral hazard, stifles innovation, and diminishes the role of personal responsibility in our economy. It is also procyclical , passes on greater costs than benefits to consumers, and needlessly restricts personal freedom.

Those who simply advocate for reregulation because they claim that the free markets have failed ignore the various ways that government itself helped set the stage for the current financial crisis. The housing sector—where the difficulties confronting our markets started—is not a deregulated, free-market in any sense of the word. This country's housing market is overloaded with substantial government components, including the regulatory roles of large government agencies; implicit and explicit government guarantees supporting the underwriting, issuance, and securitization of mortgages; and a cluster of mandates aimed at achieving universal home ownership. Indeed, the crisis this country finds itself facing does not stem from deregulation (since little has taken place over the last couple of decades) or even the mistakes of participants in the free market (although many harmful mistakes were committed), but instead from the myriad ways in which government initiatives interfered with the functioning of private markets.

Our observations have led us to conclude that there are at least five key factors that led to the current crisis:

1. A highly accommodative monetary policy that lowered interest rates dramatically, kept them low, and inflated the housing bubble.
2. Broad federal policies designed to expand home ownership in an "off-budget" fashion, which encouraged lending to those who could not afford home ownership.
3. The moral hazard inherent in Fannie Mae and Freddie Mac, the two failed GSEs, which exploited their congressionally granted duopoly status to benefit from privatized profits earned against socialized risks taken.
4. An anticompetitive government sanctioned credit rating oligopoly that misled investors and failed in its responsibility to provide accurate, transparent assessments of risk.
5. Failures throughout the mortgage securitization process that resulted in the abandonment of sound underwriting practices.

Monetary policy

The Federal Reserve set the stage for a wave of mortgage borrowing by keeping credit conditions too loose for too long earlier this decade. In response to the bursting of the high- tech bubble in 2000, the Federal Reserve began lowering interest rates in early 2001 to cushion the economic fallout. These highly accommodative policies were maintained in response to the 2001 recession and the economic shock of the 9-11 terrorist attacks. The target for the federal funds rate—the benchmark interbank lending rate in the U.S.—was lowered to just 1 percent by mid- 2003, and maintained at that level until mid-2004.[124] The real funds rate—which is the difference between the funds rate set by the Federal Reserve and expected inflation—demonstrates just how aggressively the Federal Reserve was in conducting monetary policy during this period. The real funds rate dropped from 4 percent in late 2000 to -1.5 percent by early 2003.[125]

The Federal Reserve's decision to cushion the economic blow from the dramatic collapse in equity prices unleashed a wave of cheap credit on a housing market that was already experiencing a boom cycle. By mid-2003, the interest rate on a conventional thirty-year mortgage dipped to an all-time low of just 5.25 percent, fueling demand in the housing market thanks to mortgage credit that had become cheap and plentiful in light of the Federal Reserve's rate cuts.[126] As a result of demand and cheap credit, new home construction rose to a twenty-five-year high in late 2003, and remained at historic levels for two years.[127]

It has been widely reported that over the last fifty years, there has not been a single year in which the national average home value had fallen despite some regional declines and various economic troubles and recessions. The allure of this statistic was so appealing that even former Federal Reserve Chairman Alan Greenspan and current Chairman Ben Bernanke at various points attested to it in defense of our housing markets. In fact, a 2004 report by top economists from Fannie Mae, Freddie Mac, the National Association of Realtors, the National Association of Home Builders, and the Independent Community Bankers of America entitled *America's Home Forecast: The Next Decade for Housing and Mortgage Finance* even concluded that "there is little possibility of a widespread national decline since there is no national housing market."[128] This widely held belief augmented Federal Reserve monetary policy and further inflated the housing bubble.

Even with the brisk pace of home construction, demand still outstripped supply, pushing home prices even higher. Between 1995 and 2002, in the midst of the housing boom, home prices appreciated between 2 percent and 5 percent a year. By 2004 and 2005, at the height of the bubble, home prices were appreciating at nearly 15 percent per year. Between 1997 and 2006, real home prices for the U.S. as a whole increased 85 percent. Another measure of the unsustainable inflation that took place in housing prices is the relationship between house prices and rents. Over the past twenty-five years, the price-to-rent ratio was roughly 16.5. In 2003, at the start of the bubble, the price-to-rent ratio was 18.5. It then quickly grew to an all-time peak of 25 by the end of 2005.[129]

The bubble grew as cheap credit and sharply increasing home prices fueled the frenzy of first-time homeowners eager to buy into a market before prices got out of reach. It also encouraged current homeowners to purchase bigger homes or to buy additional properties for investment purposes. Federal Reserve economists have estimated that the share of investment real estate purchases jumped to roughly 17 percent in 2005 and 2006 at the height of the housing boom, up from just more than 6 percent a decade earlier.[130]

These double digit increases in housing prices not only stimulated demand among home buyers who wanted to get into the housing market before they were priced out or were eager to invest on rising home prices, they also created an environment in which lenders, securitizers, and investors believed that it was impossible to make a bad loan. The consequences should have been foreseeable. Borrowers bought bigger, more expensive homes, betting that perpetually rising housing prices would allow them to refinance their mortgages at a later date while benefiting from ongoing appreciation in housing values. Lenders assumed that even if buyers defaulted, rising house prices would allow them to sell the home for more than the amount owed by the borrower.

Economists have consistently identified the Federal Reserve's accommodative monetary policy as one cause of the current financial crisis. For example, John B. Taylor, a professor of economics at Stanford and the creator of the "Taylor rule" guideline for monetary policy, has said the Federal Reserve made a mistake by keeping interest rates so low. According to Taylor's formula, the Federal Reserve should have raised interest rates much sooner than it did given the economic conditions at the time. Taylor himself has said that "a higher funds path would have avoided much of the housing boom.... The reversal of the boom and thereby the resulting market turmoil would not have been as sharp."[131] Given the key role that the Federal Reserve's monetary policy has played in contributing to the credit crisis we now face, it must be acknowledged that those decisions had a major impact on market conditions and helped to influence how investors chose to allocate their capital in our economy.

Federal policy to expand home ownership

For well over twenty years, federal policy has promoted lending and borrowing to expand homeownership, through incentives such as the home mortgage interest tax exclusion, the Federal Housing Administration (FHA), and discretionary spending programs such as HUD's HOME block grant program. But perhaps the most damaging initiative undertaken by the federal government was the effort to pressure private financial institutions to subsidize home ownership through the Community Reinvestment Act (CRA). Undertaken with the best of intentions—expanding home ownership among poor and underserved communities—the unintended consequences of the CRA clearly demonstrate that government's attempts to manipulate market behavior to achieve social goals often lead to harmful results.

Enacted in 1977, the CRA encouraged banks to extend credit to "underserved" populations by requiring that banks insured by the federal government "help meet the credit needs of its entire community." To ensure that banks are meeting this mandate, each federally insured bank is periodically examined by its federal regulator. As a result of its enactment, bank lending to low- and moderate-income families has increased by 80 percent.[132]

In 1997, Wall Street firms, the GSEs, and the CRA converged in a landmark event: the first securitization of CRA loans, a $384-million offering guaranteed by Freddie Mac.[133] Over the next 10 months, Bear Stearns issued $1.9 billion of CRA mortgages, backed by Fannie or Freddie, and between 2000 and 2002 this business accelerated in dramatic fashion as Fannie Mae issued $20 billion in securities backed by CRA mortgages.[134] By encouraging lenders and underwriters to relax their traditional underwriting practices, the CRA, investment firms and the GSEs saddled American taxpayers with the consequences of mortgages that borrowers cannot repay.

Equally problematic are reports that some of these CRA-inspired loans are mortgages that borrowers can repay, but choose not to, given that the property that secures these loans is now worth less than the amount outstanding. Whether borrowers cannot or will not repay, the irony is that these lower-income home buyers—those who were supposed to benefit from the government's actions— are now defaulting at a rate three times that of other borrowers. With these defaults, the damage to homeowners, neighborhoods, state and local governments as the tax base shrinks, and now to all American taxpayers, is enormous.

In the course of this crisis, there has been some heated discussion over the role CRA loans have played in contributing to our current woes. Proponents of CRA-like mandates have maintained that only a small portion of subprime mortgage originations are related to the CRA, and those CRA loans that have been written are performing in a manner similar to other types of subprime loans. Such claims, however, miss the fundamental point that critics of the CRA have made: though they may be small in volume, CRA loan mandates remain large in precedent because they inherently required lending institutions to abandon their traditional underwriting standards in favor of more subjective models to meet their government mandated CRA obligations.

For example, in April of 1993, the Boston Federal Reserve Bank, under the leadership of future Freddie Mac Chairman Dick Syron, published an influential best practices guide called *Closing the Gap: A Guide To Equal Opportunity Lending*. The guide made several recommendations to lending institutions on various ways they could increase their low-income lending practices. Some of these recommendations, which encouraged institutions to abandon the traditional lending and underwriting policies used to ensure the quality of loans made, included:

1. "Special care should be taken to ensure that standards are appropriate to the economic culture of urban, lower-income, and nontraditional consumers."
2. "Policies regarding applicants with no credit history or problem credit history should be reviewed. Lack of credit history should not be seen as a negative factor.... In reviewing past credit problems, lenders should be willing to consider extenuating circumstances."
3. Institutions can "work with the public sector to develop products that assist lower-income borrowers by using public money to reduce interest rates, provide down payment assistance, or otherwise reduce the cost of the mortgage."
4. "A prompt and impartial second review of all rejected applications can help ensure fairness in the lending decision and prevent the loss of business opportunities.... This process may lead to changes in the institution's underwriting policies.... In addition, loan production staff may find that their experience with minority applicants indicates that the institution's stated loan policy should be modified to incorporate some of the allowable compensating factors."[135]

Taken in isolation, the good intentions of these recommendations is plain; taken together, however, it is also clear that lenders were being urged to abandon proven safety and soundness underwriting standards in favor of new outcome-based underwriting standards. Again, the salient point is not to debate the notion of could or should more be done to make affordable loans available to underserved communities. The question is what damage is done to the overall stability of an institution when it alters its lending guidelines to comply with a government mandate to advance a social policy.

Similarly, banks were urged by other private sector parties to ignore traditional lending guidelines, this time in the pursuit of greater and faster profit. In May of 1998, Bear Stearns published an article with guidance on why and how lenders should package CRA loans into mortgage backed securities.[136] That document advised lenders that: "Traditionally rating agencies view LTV [loan-tovalue ratios] as the single most important determinant of default. It is most important at the time of origination and less so after the third year." Bear Stearns also encouraged lower lending standards by arguing that when "explaining the credit quality of a portfolio to a rating agency or GSE, it is essential to go beyond credit scores," and that "the use of default models traditionally used for conforming loans have to be adjusted for CRA affordable loans." While such advice might have been important to maximizing profitability, Bear Stearns' guidance is yet one more example of how the conflict between a social policy mandate like the CRA and the fiscal requirements of basic safety and soundness operations led to a dangerous diminution in lenders' traditional underwriting standards.

The GSEs

Standing at the center of the American system of mortgage finance are the two now- failed government-chartered behemoths created to expand homeownership opportunities: the Federal National Mortgage Association (Fannie Mae) and the Federal Home Loan Mortgage Corporation (Freddie Mac). Market participants have long understood that this government created duopoly was implicitly, though not explicitly, backed by the federal government. This "implied guarantee" flowed from several factors, including the very existence of a government charter that effectively sanctioned this duopoly, access to a Treasury line of credit, and exemption from payment of state and local taxes. Although Fannie and Freddie were nominally designed to be competitors, in practice this implied guarantee allowed the two largely to work in unison as a cartel to set and maintain prices in the market.

The dangers inherent in such an implied guarantee were twofold. First, their unique status allowed Fannie and Freddie to borrow funds in the marketplace at subsidized rates. Ostensibly, these funds would be used to purchase mortgages from lenders, fulfilling their mission to provide liquidity in the secondary mortgage markets. For over a decade, however, the GSEs continued to build enormous investment portfolios, earning profits by arbitraging the difference between their low, subsidized borrowing costs and the higher yields in their portfolio's ever riskier assets. Beginning in 1990, their investment portfolios grew tenfold, from $135 billion to $1.5 trillion,[137] allowing many of their shareholders and executives to become personally wealthy thanks to the GSEs' subsidized borrowing costs while the American taxpayer assumed most of the risk.

Second, their implied guarantee created a false sense of security and standards for the products they purchased and securitized. This perception played a major role in the proliferation of GSE-backed subprime and Alt-A securities, providing a *de facto* government seal of approval for even the riskiest loans as market participants believed these securities were appropriately priced and represented minimal risk. Their predominance in the mortgage market meant that Fannie and Freddie's business practices—credit rating, underwriting, risk modeling—were seen as the "gold standard" in the industry, despite flaws that later became apparent.

For its part, Congress substantially magnified these potential risks by charging the GSEs with a mission to promote homeownership and thus inflating the supply of credit available to fund residential mortgages. The GSEs' congressional mandate and their access to cheap funding allowed the government to pressure Fannie and Freddie to expand homeownership to historically credit- risky individuals without the burden of an explicit on-budget line item at taxpayer expense, a budget goal long sought by housing advocates. For instance, in 1996, the HUD required that 42 percent of Fannie's and Freddie's mortgage financing should go to borrowers with income levels below the median for a given area.[138] HUD revised those goals again in 2004, increasing them to 56 percent of their overall mortgage purchases by 2008.[139] In addition, HUD required that 12 percent of all mortgage *purchases* by Fannie and Freddie be "special affordable" loans made to borrowers with incomes less than 60 percent of an area's median income, and ultimately increased that target to 28 percent for 2008.[140]

These "affordable housing" goals and other federal policies succeeded at increasing the homeownership rate from 64 percent in 1994 to an all-time high of 69 percent in 2005.[141] However, they did so at a great cost. To meet these increasingly large government mandates, Fannie and Freddie began to buy riskier loans and encouraged those who might not be ready to buy homes to take out mortgages. This GSE-manufactured demand boosted home prices to an artificially high level and fostered enthusiasm for the wave of exotic mortgage products that began to flood the market.

For example, in 1999, under pressure from the Clinton Administration to expand home loans among low- and moderate-income groups, Fannie Mae introduced a pilot program in fifteen major markets encouraging banks to extend mortgage credit to persons who lacked the proper credit histories to qualify for conventional loans. The risks of such a program should have been apparent to all. *The New York Times*, in a prescient comment on the program at the time, remarked: "In moving, even tentatively, into this new area of lending, Fannie Mae is taking on significantly more risk, which may not pose any difficulties during flush economic times. But the government-subsidized corporation may run into trouble in an economic downturn, prompting an economic rescue."[142]

During this period, the government also began to push Fannie and Freddie into the subprime market. In 1995, HUD authorized Fannie and Freddie to purchase subprime securities that included loans to low-income borrowers and allowed the GSEs to receive credit for those loans toward their mandatory affordable housing goals. Subprime lending, it was thought, would benefit many borrowers who did not qualify for conventional loans. Fannie and Freddie readily complied, and as a result, subprime and near-prime loans jumped from 9 percent of securitized mortgages in 2001 to 40 percent in 2006.[143]

Fannie's and Freddie's heavy involvement in subprime and Alt-A mortgages increased following their accounting scandals in 2003 and 2004 in an attempt to curry favor with Congress and avoid stricter regulation. Data from these critical years before the housing crisis hit show Fannie and Freddie had a large direct and indirect role in the market for risky mortgage loans. In 2004 alone, Fannie and Freddie purchased $175 billion in subprime mortgage securities, which accounted for 44 percent of the market that year. Then, from 2005 through 2007, the two GSEs purchased approximately $1 trillion in subprime and Alt-A loans, and Fannie's acquisitions of mortgages with less than 10-percent down payments almost tripled.[144]

Without question, the purchase and securitization of such loans by Fannie and Freddie was a clear signal and incentive to all loan originators to write more subprime and Alt-A loans regardless of their quality. As a result, the market share of conventional mortgages dropped from 78.8 percent in 2003 to 50.1 percent by 2007 with a corresponding increase in subprime and Alt-A loans from 10.1 percent to 32.7 percent over the same period.[145] The message, as *The New York Times* noted, was clear: "[T]he ripple effect of Fannie's plunge into riskier lending was profound. Fannie's stamp of approval made shunned borrowers and complex loans more acceptable to other lenders, particularly small and less sophisticated banks."[146] Soon, Fannie and Freddie became the largest purchasers of the higher-rated (AAA) tranches of the subprime pools that were securitized by the market. This support was essential both to form these investment pools and market them around the world. Fannie and Freddie thus played a pivotal role in the growth and diffusion of the mortgage securities that are now crippling our financial system.

Fannie and Freddie also played a leading role in weakening the underwriting standards that had previously helped ensure that borrowers would repay their mortgages. For instance, in May 2008, Fannie and Freddie relaxed the down payment criteria on the mortgages they buy, accepting loans with down payments as low as 3 percent.[147] And in recent years both companies markedly stepped up their guarantees on Alt-A loans, which often did not require the verification of income, savings, or assets for potential borrowers. Between 2005 and the first half of 2008, Fannie guaranteed at least $230 billion worth of these risky loans, more than three times the amount it had guaranteed on all past years combined. However, these poorly underwritten loans are now increasingly turning sour amid the housing downturn, especially those concentrated in California, Florida, Nevada, and Arizona, where the housing bubble was particularly large and real estate speculation was rampant.[148]

To preserve their government-granted duopoly powers and maintain unfettered access to cheap funds, Fannie and Freddie spent enormous sums on lobbying and public relations. According to the *Associated Press*, they "tenaciously worked to nurture, and then protect, their financial empires by invoking the political sacred cow of homeownership and fielding an army of lobbyists, power brokers and political contributors."[149] Fannie and Freddie's lobbyists fought off legislation that might shrink their investment portfolios or erode their ties to the federal government, raising their borrowing costs. In fact, Franklin D. Raines, Fannie Mae's former chairman, once told an investor conference that "we manage our political risk with the same intensity that we manage our credit and interest rate risk."[150] Raines's statement was undoubtedly true: over the past ten years, Fannie and Freddie spent more than $174 million on lobbying.[151]

As long as times were good, the GSEs were able to point to their affordable housing goals to distract attention from the inherent risk their business model posed. But, for more than a decade, alarms have been sounded about the precarious position of the GSEs. For example, in Congress, as far back as 1998, GSE reform advocates like former Rep. Richard Baker were voicing their concerns over "the risks and potential liabilities that GSEs represent."[152] In 2000, Rep. Baker demonstrated he was far ahead of the curve when he observed that by "improving the existing regulatory structure of the housing GSEs in today's good economic climate, we can reduce future risk to the taxpayer and the economy."[153] That year, the House Financial Services Committee held no fewer than six hearings on the subject of GSE reform, with at least five more over the following two years.[154] Yet from 2000 to 2005, although at least eight major GSE reform bills were introduced in Congress, Fannie and Freddie exerted enough influence that only one, the Federal

Housing Finance Reform Act of 2005, ever gained enough support to be passed by either body, but it ultimately did not become law.[155]

Others in government shared similar concerns. In 1997, the General Accountability Office cautioned in its testimony before the House Financial Services Committee that "the outstanding volume of federally assisted GSE credit is large and rapidly increasing."[156] As referenced above, then-Treasury Under Secretary Gensler testified in March 2000 that "the willingness of a GSE to purchase a mortgage has become a far more significant factor in deciding whether to originate that mortgage." Gensler went on to state that as the GSEs continue to grow, "issues of potential systemic risk and market competition become more relevant," and concluded that the current moment was "an ideal time to review the supervision and regulation of the GSEs."[157] In 2004, then-Federal Reserve Chairman Alan Greenspan warned in his testimony before the Senate Banking, Housing, and Urban Affairs Committee that "the current system depends on the risk managers at Fannie and Freddie to do everything just right.... But to fend off possible future systemic difficulties, which we assess as likely if GSE expansion continues unabated, preventive actions are required sooner rather than later."[158]

Outside of Congress, more red flags were flown over the obvious weaknesses of the GSE model. At another House Financial Services Committee hearing on GSEs in 2000, low-income housing advocate John Taylor of the National Community Reinvestment Coalition warned that the lack of a strong regulatory agency for Fannie and Freddie "threatens the safety and soundness of the GSEs."[159] At the same hearing, community activist Bruce Marks of the Neighborhood Assistance Corporation of America expressed his fears that without enhanced regulatory control over Fannie and Freddie, the GSEs might participate "in potentially profitable but also potentially risky investments [*sic*] schemes [that] pose potential risks for the housing and banking industry and for the economy in general."[160]

Unfortunately, despite all the evidence of systemic risk and repeated efforts to consolidate, strengthen, and increase regulatory oversight of Fannie and Freddie, calls for reform mostly fell on deaf ears. One reason why reform efforts failed was that the GSEs and their ardent defenders in Congress have spent the better part of the last decade first ignoring, then rejecting, then attempting to contradict the mounting evidence that the whole system was in danger. In 2001, Fannie Mae itself attempted to dispel the need for any change, declaring before Congress that "we operate successfully under the most rigorous of safety and soundness regimes; we are subject to a high level of market discipline and provide the marketplace with world-class disclosures."[161] Freddie Mac, for its part, used the same hearing to proclaim that their "superior risk management capabilities, strong capital position and state-of-the-art information disclosure make Freddie Mac unquestionably a safe and sound financial institution."[162]

After their credibility eroded from their accounting scandals, Fannie and Freddie increasingly relied on elected officials to fight attempts at reform. In 2003, Rep. Barney Frank famously remarked at a hearing on a pending GSE reform bill: "I believe there has been more alarm raised about potential [GSE] un-safety and unsoundness than, in fact, exists.... I do not want the same kind of focus on safety and soundness that we have in OCC and OTS. I want to roll the dice a little bit more in this situation towards subsidized housing."[163] In 2004, Senator Chris Dodd called Fannie and Freddie "one of the great success stories of all time,"[164] while in 2005 Senator Chuck Schumer confessed that perhaps "Fannie and Freddie need some changes, but I don't think they need dramatic restructuring in terms of their mission."[165] The scope of this head-in-the-sand mentality was perhaps most completely embodied by Rep. Maxine Waters who, in 2002, categorically rejected the need for any GSE reform bill, proclaiming at a House Financial Services Committee hearing on the matter "If it is not broken, why fix it?"[166]

Although it is fair to say that no one ought to be blamed for lacking the ability to predict the future, the fact remains that for more than a decade there were clear, discernable, and announced warnings that Fannie and Freddie were growing too big and that if left unchecked would eventually collapse beneath their own weight. Too many public policy makers failed to heed those warnings, or knowingly disregarded them, and as a result taxpayers have now been left to pick up the pieces by taking on hundreds of billions of dollars worth of risk. Ironically, when the housing bubble finally burst, the resulting wave of foreclosures stemming from loans the GSEs forced into the market will likely end up reducing homeownership rates across the country, a direct contradiction to the stated purpose of Fannie and Freddie that their supporters for so long sought to advance.

Credit rating agencies

In order to sell subprime securities to investors, those securities first had to be rated by the credit rating agencies. Like so many other players, the credit rating agencies were caught up in the pursuit of fees generated from the real estate boom. This overwhelming desire to maximize their profits from the housing bubble is perhaps best captured by an e-mail message from a Standard & Poor's official who wrote that "We rate every deal. It could be structured by cows and we would rate it."[167] To perform their work, these agencies made extensive use of sophisticated modeling in an attempt to predict risk and the likelihood of default on loans. However, much like everyone else, the credit rating agencies falsely assumed that housing prices would never go down nationwide, which meant that their elaborate mathematical models were defective from the start. When mortgage defaults accelerated and home prices began to plummet, securities based on those loans that were once highly rated were downgraded to junk causing a wave of financial turmoil for scores of market participants at every level.

But the failure of the credit rating agencies would not have generated the disastrous consequences that it did had that failure not been compounded by further misguided government policies, which had effectively allowed the credit rating agencies to operate as a cartel. For decades, federal financial regulators have required that regulated entities heed the ratings of a select few rating agencies. For example, since the 1930s regulators have not allowed banks to invest in bonds that are below "investment grade," as determined by the select few rating agencies as recognized by the government. Although the goal of having safe bonds in the portfolios of banks may be a worthy one, bank regulators essentially delegated a major portion of their safety assessments to the opinions of these rating agencies.

This delegation of authority by bank regulators was further compounded in 1975, when the SEC also delegated its safety judgments regarding broker-dealers to the credit rating agencies. As an attempted safeguard against unqualified agencies from participating in the process, the SEC created a new Nationally Recognized Statistical Rating Organization (NRSRO) designation for qualified entities, and immediately grandfathered the three large rating agencies into this category. Following the SEC, other financial regulators soon adopted the NRSRO category for their delegations, assuming this government stamp of approval would ensure the continued quality of the ratings produced by those agencies.

Over the next 25 years, the SEC allowed only four more rating firms to achieve the NRSRO designation, but mergers among the NRSROs eligible to issue ratings recognized by the regulators shrunk the number of NRSROs back to three by year-end 2000. In 2006, Congress passed legislation (Pub. L. No. 109-29 1) to address part of this situation which required that the SEC cease being a barrier to entry for legitimate rating agencies, and gave it limited regulatory powers over the NRSROs. Although the SEC has designated six additional NRSROs since 2000,[168] competition and transparency in the ratings agency system remains inadequate. The SEC has never developed criteria for the designation and, once designated, NRSROs have for too long been allowed to operate without further scrutiny by the SEC for competence or accuracy.

By adopting this NRSRO system, the SEC thus established an insurmountable barrier to entry into the rating business, eliminating market competition among the rating agencies. No one could be surprised that once they were spared the market discipline, the quality of the work by protected rating agencies would diminish.

Market behavior

Government policies that dominated and distorted the nation's housing market clearly set the stage for the housing crisis. But there were also significant mistakes made by private- sector participants at each step of the originate-to-distribute model of mortgage financing which compounded the government's failure. The benefits of this system—such a lower financing costs and the efficient distribution of risk—were significant. Over time, however, the belief that home prices would continue their relentless, upward path distorted began to distort decision making at every step along the path.

The belief that real estate prices would only go up led borrowers, originators, lenders, securitizers, and investors to conclude that these investments were risk free. As a result, the traditional underwriting standards, based on the borrower's character, capacity to repay, and the quality of collateral were abandoned. What many failed to realize was that those standards were designed not only to protect the participants in the system from the consequences of a bubble, but also to protect the underlying financial system itself.

Borrowers. Building on that belief that housing prices could never go down, borrowers were encouraged to borrow as much as possible and buy as much house as they possible could, or else invest in other properties that could always later be resold for a profit. The result was that borrowers often ended up with mortgage products that they failed to understand, that they could not afford, or that ended up exceeding the value of the property securing the mortgage. Those concerns were less important as property values continued to rise, since borrowers could always refinance or sell to benefit from the continued appreciation of the property. However, when property values began to fall, in many cases borrowers soon realized that the economically rational course of action for them was to mail in their keys to the mortgage servicer and simply walk away. Since mortgages are non- recourse loans, doing so meant that someone else was bearing the downside risk. While the vast majority of borrowers continue to honor their commitments and pay their mortgages, for many of those who put little or no money down their mortgages became a "heads I win, tails you lose" proposition.

Mortgage originators. Because mortgage originators were compensated on the quantity rather than the quality of loans they originated, there was little incentive to care if the loans they originated would perform. The compensation of mortgage brokers was also tied to the interest rates and fees paid by customers, which created a financial incentive for some brokers to direct borrowers to loans that may not have otherwise been in their best interest. For example, some originators who advocated for certain subprime loans received commissions that were more than twice as high as the commissions they would have received for higher-quality loans. This incentives model put a much higher premium on quantity over quality, which only diminished the safety and soundness of the entire system as even more risks were externalized while profits were internalized.

Mortgage fraud. Integral to understanding the root causes of our current credit crisis is an acknowledgement of the rampant mortgage fraud that took place in the mortgage industry during the boom years. Fueled by low interest rates and soaring home values, the mortgage industry soon attracted both unscrupulous originators as well as disingenuous borrowers, resulting in billions of dollars in losses. As early as 2004, FBI officials in charge of criminal investigations foresaw that mortgage fraud had the potential to mushroom into an epidemic. In 2008, the Department of Treasury's Financial Crimes Enforcement Network (FinCEN) announced a 44 percent increase in Suspicious Activity Reports from financial institutions reporting mortgage fraud, with some 37,313 mortgage fraud reports filed in 2006, and 52,868 mortgage fraud reports filed in 2007. According to FinCEN, mortgage loan fraud was the third most prevalent type of suspicious activity reported, lagging behind only money laundering and check fraud. From 2000 to 2007, FinCEN found that the reporting of suspected mortgage loan fraud had increased an astounding 1400 percent from 3,515 cases in 2000 to 52,868 cases in 2007.[169]

Unfortunately, law enforcement officials failed to stop the epidemic that they had accurately diagnosed because they did not devote adequate resources to the problem. Even though the FBI and the Justice Department are charged with the responsibility of investigating and prosecuting illegal activities by originators, lenders, and borrowers, the focus of those agencies was trained on national security and other priorities. As a result, inadequate attention was paid to many of the white-collar crimes that contributed to the financial crisis. For example, by 2007, the number of agents pursuing mortgage fraud shrank to around 100.[170] By comparison, the FBI had about a thousand agents deployed on banking fraud during the S&L bust of the 1980s and 1990s. Although the FBI later increased the number of agents working on mortgage fraud to 200, others have pointed out that the agency might have averted much of the problem had it heeded its own warning about widespread mortgage fraud.[171]

Lenders. The belief that housing prices would rise forever, coupled with the ability to package loans for sale to investors, profoundly changed the way in which lenders underwrote loans. While underwriting had traditionally been based on the borrower's ability to repay a loan, as measured by criteria such as employment history, income, down payment, credit rating, and loan-to-value ratios, rising home prices pushed lenders to abandon these criteria. Little concern was paid to the risks of this change, given that in a worst-case scenario, servicers could always foreclose upon a property to satisfy the mortgage in full. As a result, lenders pioneered new mortgage products, such as no-doc and low-doc loans, low- and no-down-payment loans, and innovations that took rising home prices for granted. That is not to say that these exotic products are illegitimate; each may have its own appropriate use for borrowers in specific circumstances. But the broad application of these tailored products to *any* person in *any* circumstance invariably led to some borrowers receiving loans that were wholly inappropriate for their needs and capacity to repay. The ability to securitize these loans further degraded lending standards by allowing lenders to shift the risk of nonperforming mortgages onto the investors that purchased securities built around these products. In a world in which lenders could securitize even the most poorly underwritten of mortgages, what mattered most to lenders was that the loan did not default within an agreed-upon period—typically 90 or 180 days. Whatever happened after that time was someone else's problem.

Securitizers. Securitizers pooled mortgages of all types and quality together to create complex and often opaque structured products from these loans, such as mortgage-backed securities (MBS) and collateralized debt obligations (CDO). Securitizers knew that some portion of the mortgages they securitized would fail, but they believed that by structuring these mortgages into securities with different levels of risk, they could effectively eliminate any risk from those defaults with the guarantee of safer, performing loans. This belief grew from the assumption that others along the chain—the mortgage brokers and lenders—had adequately underwritten the loans so that any defaults would be manageable, and that housing prices would never go down. Those false assumptions belied the fact remains that in any finance model, you can never eliminate risk from a system of lending; at best, you can hope to control it by offsetting smaller sections of riskier loans with larger sections of safer loans. But that risk, while controlled, is always there, a lesson which the entire financial system is currently experiencing firsthand.

Investors. Like so many others, private investors in pursuit of risk-free investments failed to appreciate that if housing prices could go up, they could also go down. Rather than performing their due diligence on these mortgage-backed securities, many investors put their faith in the rating agencies and other proxies, and did not fully appreciate the risks they faced. Some large institutions further compounded their mistakes by holding their mortgage investments off-balance-sheet, using a loophole set forth in the regulatory capital requirements that permitted them to hold low-risk investments in special investment vehicles or conduits. And other large institutions—such as the former investment banks—availed themselves of an exemption granted by the SEC that permitted them to ignore traditional debt-to-net capital ratios—traditionally 12: 1—and lever up as much as 40:1.[172] It was in this way that the once highly sought but ultimately poorly underwritten mortgages came to be the "troubled assets" that have now caused the collapse of so many in our financial system. Using first the assumption, and by 2008 the proof, that the government would deem certain institutions that had gambled on these assets to be too big or too interconnected to fail, these institutions and their creditors succeeded in making the taxpayer the ultimate bag holder for the risks they took, demonstrating yet again that the standard governing the housing boom and bust was "heads I win, tails you lose."

Mark-to-Market Accounting. The boom and bust nature of the housing and financial markets in recent years was amplified by the application of financial accounting standards that required financial institutions to write down their MBS assets to "market value" even if no market existed. As a result, institutions that held mortgage-backed securities found themselves facing the withdrawal of financing, often forcing them to sell these assets at distressed or liquidation prices, even though the underlying cash flows of these portfolios might not have been seriously diminished. In a liquidity-starved market, more and more distressed sales took place, further pulling down asset prices. These declining prices in turn created more lender demands for additional collateral to secure their loans, which in turn resulted in more distressed sales and further declines in asset values as measured on a mark-to-market basis. The result was a procyclical engine which magnified every downward price change in a recursive spiral, all of which might have otherwise been avoided had the mark-to-market standard provided better guidance on how to value assets in non-functioning markets.

Summary. The financial crisis which has unfolded over the past two years has numerous causes, and decisions made in the private sector were, in many cases, unwise. But the failure of government policy and the market distortions it caused stand at the center of the crisis. Whether by the Federal Reserve's engineering an artificially low interest rate, Congress's well-intentioned but misguided efforts to expand home ownership among less creditworthy borrowers, or the GSEs' securitization and purchase of risky mortgage-backed securities, the federal government bears a significant share of the responsibility for the challenges that confront us today.

To address these challenges, what is needed most is not simply reregulation or expanded regulation, but a modernized regulatory system that is appropriate to the size, global reach, and technology used by today's most sophisticated financial service firms. At a time when our nation's economy desperately needs to attract new investment and restore the flow of credit to where it can be used most productively, we must at all costs avoid regulatory changes under the label "reform" that have the unintended consequence of further destabilizing or constricting our economy. We should carefully consider the so-called lessons of the subprime crisis to be sure that whatever changes we adopt actually address the specific underlying causes of the crisis. These reforms should require the participants in the financial system to bear the full costs of their decisions, just as they enjoy the benefits. They should also enhance market forces, add increased transparency, and strip away counterproductive government mandates.

Perhaps above all, we should avoid creating a system in which market participants rely upon an implicit or explicit government guarantee to bear the risk for economic transactions gone wrong. If the events of the past two years have demonstrated anything, it is that whenever government attempts to subsidize risk—from efforts to stabilize home prices to the latest government-engineered rescues of financial institutions deemed too big to fail—those efforts are usually costly, typically ineffectual, and often counterproductive. We should all know by now that whenever government subsidizes risk, either by immunizing parties from the consequences of their behavior or allowing them to shift risk to others at no cost, we produce a clear moral hazard that furthers risky behavior, usually with disastrous consequences.

Any regulatory reform program must recognize the ways in which government is part of the problem, and should guard against an overreaction that is certain to have unintended consequences. Perhaps Harvard economist Edward L. Glaeser put it best: "We do need new and better regulations, but the current public mood seems to be guided more by a taste for vengeance than by a rational desire to weigh costs and benefits. Before imposing new rules, we need to think clearly about what those rules are meant to achieve and impose only those regulations that will lead our financial markets to function better."[173]

Recommendations for Federal Regulatory Reform

Developing an agenda for reform is an inherently controversial enterprise. As with any suggested change, some will stand to benefit while others might be forced to adjust to the new realities of a different regulatory scheme. The recommendations contained here are not immune from this charge, and there will invariably be disagreement over the advantages and disadvantages of some of these proposals. However, we believe that the following recommendations remain true to our objectives of helping to make markets more competitive and transparent, empowering consumers with effective disclosure to make rational decisions, effectively policing markets for force and fraud, and reducing systemic risk.

In considering the appropriateness of each item, the devil will always be in the details regarding how any of these recommendations might be enacted. Even the best idea, if poorly implemented, would lose many of the potential benefits it might otherwise yield. Thus, these recommendations are best understood as conceptual proposals rather than specific instructions for how to improve our regulatory system.

Given the limited time and resources available to the Panel to conduct this review, in many cases there are still unanswered questions about certain aspects of these reforms and in some cases even a few qualified reservations between the authors. Nevertheless, we believe that each proposal contains clear benefits for our economy, and has been structured to avoid the potential for unintended consequences. They deserve open consideration and debate in the public arena, and the opportunity to stand or fall on their own merits—a fitting tribute to the competitive free-market system that we are dedicated to strengthening and preserving.

1. Reform the Mortgage Finance System

The current financial crisis originated in the mortgage finance system, and much of the resulting turmoil can be traced to government interventions in the housing sector which helped fuel a classic asset bubble. Reform must begin with Fannie Mae and Freddie Mac, the GSEs whose influence drove the deterioration of underwriting standards, growth in subprime mortgage backed securities, and whose subsidized structure will result in hundreds of billions of dollars in taxpayer losses. The mortgage origination market itself should also be improved by establishing clearer standards, transparency, and enforcement.

1.1. Re-charter the housing GSEs as mortgage guarantors, removing them from the investment business

At the center of the need for reform are Fannie Mae and Freddie Mac. As Charles Calomiris and Peter Wallison of AEI recently wrote: "Many monumental errors and misjudgments contributed to the acute financial turmoil in which we now find ourselves. Nevertheless, the vast accumulation of toxic mortgage debt that poisoned the global financial system was driven by the aggressive buying of subprime and Alt-A mortgages, and mortgage-backed securities, by Fannie Mae and Freddie Mac. The poor choices of these two GSEs—and their sponsors in Washington—are largely to blame for our current mess."[174]

The GSEs fueled the housing bubble through their ever expanding appetite for increasingly risky investments that they held in their massive portfolios. They financed these investments by borrowing at low, subsidized rates, and over time the firms became ever more dependent on their high yields to meet their earning targets. At one time, Fannie and Freddie accounted for more default risk than all other U.S. corporations combined—default risk implicitly backed by the federal government.[175] These risks to the taxpayer and the financial system were obvious, and should have been dealt with long ago.

Now that the GSEs have been taken into conservatorship, Congress has the opportunity to ensure that the damage they inflicted will never be repeated. This can be accomplished in one of two ways. One option is for Congress to phase out the GSEs' government charter and privatize them over a reasonable period of time following a model similar to that of the successful Sallie Mae privatization a decade ago. Legislation to that effect was introduced in the 110th Congress and will likely be re-introduced in the current Congress. These firms can and should compete effectively in the financial service marketplace on a level playing field without implicit or explicit taxpayer guarantees.

Alternatively, Congress could opt to recharter the GSEs as government entities whose only mandate is to guarantee and help securitize mortgages. Such a structure would remove them entirely from the investment business by prohibiting them from maintaining massive investment portfolios which have proven to be a tremendous source of systemic risk. In either alternative, Congress must avoid a return to the flawed public purpose/private ownership model that permitted the GSEs' shareholders to profit at taxpayer expense.

1.2. Simplify mortgage disclosure

The events of the past year have made painfully clear that the vitality of our financial system depends on a well-functioning housing market in which borrowers are able and willing to abide by the terms of the mortgage contracts into which they have entered. Unfortunately, the needless complexity involved in obtaining a mortgage appears designed to keep borrowers from fully understanding these important agreements. One way to minimize this complexity is to place essential information for borrowers in a simple, one-page document that makes clear what borrowers need to know before they enter into what will be for many the biggest financial transaction they will ever undertake. This information will permit borrowers to make an appropriate decision regarding the costs and affordability of borrowing to buy a house. This one-page document would include such items as monthly payments, interest rate, fees, and possible changes in the amount of payments for adjustable rate mortgages including the maximum possible interest rate on the loan and the maximum monthly payment in dollars. The one-page document should also include the warning that home values can go down as well as up, and that the consumer is responsible for making the mortgage payments even when the price goes down.

1.3. Establish minimum equity requirements for government guaranteed mortgages

Because federally guaranteed mortgages put the taxpayer on the hook for any potential associated losses, the taxpayer needs to be protected from opportunistic borrowers that might otherwise walk away from a mortgage if housing prices fall. One way to protect the taxpayer is require the borrower to provide a bigger downpayment. If the taxpayer is going to take on risk, it is only fair that the borrower share in that risk as well.

FHA loans currently require at least a 3.5 percent downpayment, which is clearly too low. The minimum downpayment for all government-insured or securitized mortgages should be raised immediately to at least 5 percent, and to as much as 10 percent or higher, over the next several years as market conditions improve. Lest the advocates of government-subsidized mortgages in which taxpayers bear the risk complain that 5 percent is too high, it bears pointing out that would still be *four times* as lenient as the 20 percent standard that was in place two decades ago.

1.4. Allow Federal Reserve mortgage lending rules to take effect and clarify the enforcement authority for mortgage origination standards

In July 2008, the Federal Reserve approved a comprehensive final rule for home mortgage loans that was designed to improve lending and disclosure practices. The new Federal Reserve rule was designed to prohibit unfair, abusive or deceptive home mortgage lending practices, and it applies to all mortgage lenders, not just those supervised and examined by the Federal Reserve.

The final Federal Reserve rule adds four protections for "higher priced mortgage loans," which encompasses virtually all subprime loans. The final rule:

1. Prohibits lenders from making loans without regard to a borrower's ability to repay the loan.
2. Requires creditors to verify borrowers' income and assets.
3. Bans prepayment penalties for loans in which the payment can change during the first four years of the loan (for other higher-priced loans, a prepayment penalty period cannot last for more than two years).
4. Requires creditors to establish escrow accounts for property taxes and homeowner's insurance for all first-lien mortgage loans.

In addition, the Federal Reserve issued the following protections for all loans secured by a consumer's principal dwelling:

1. Creditors and mortgage brokers are prohibited from coercing a real estate appraiser to misstate a home's value.
2. Companies that service mortgage loans are prohibited from engaging in certain practices, such as pyramiding late fees.
3. Servicers are required to credit consumers' loan payments as of the date of receipt and provide a payoff statement within a reasonable time of request.

4. Creditors must provide a good faith estimate of the loan costs, including a schedule of payments, within three days of a consumer applying for a mortgage loan.

Finally, the rule sets new advertising standards, which require additional information about rates, monthly payments, and other loan features. It also bans seven advertising practices it considers deceptive or misleading, including representing that a rate or payment is "fixed" when it can change.

These new rules represent a change in federal regulation that, regardless of whether or not one agrees with the degree to which consumers might benefit from all of these rules, will significantly alter the way in which the mortgage lending industry operates. Thus, before policymakers succumb to the desire to write additional rules and regulations, they should allow the Federal Reserve's new guidelines to take effect, monitor their impact upon mortgage origination, and clarify the authority for enforcing these new federal standards. Additionally, for these new rules to work effectively, they must be appropriately enforced. In particular, Congress should ensure that federal and state authorities have the appropriate powers to enforce these laws, both in terms of resources and actual manpower, for all mortgage originators.

1.5. Enhance securitization accountability standards

The advent of securitization has been a tremendous boon to the mortgage industry, and countless millions of Americans have directly or indirectly benefited from the liquidity it has created. Nevertheless, the communicative nature of loans in the securitization process has helped diminish accountability among market participants, eroding the quality of many loans. Thus, to restore accountability, minimum standards should be set for all loans that are to be securitized so that securitizers retain some risk for nonperforming loans.

One proposal would be to link the compensation securitizers receive for packaging loans into mortgage-backed securities to the performance of those loans over a five year period, rather than the six-month put-back period that is the current standard. This change in compensation would thus give the securitizer an economic stake in the loan's long-term performance, aligning the securitizer's incentives with those of borrowers, investors, and the broader economy. Further, consideration should be given to applying additional limitations on the ability to securitize loans that carry with them an explicit government guarantee.

2. Modernize the Regulatory Structure for Financial Institutions

It has become a cliché to observe that if one were designing a regulatory system from scratch, one would not come up with the patchwork system of agencies with overlapping jurisdictions and conflicting mandates. The U.S. financial regulatory system is fractured among eleven federal primary regulatory agencies in addition to scores of state regulatory agencies. The system developed over a 200-year period, during which institutions largely lacked the ability to transact business nationwide, let alone globally. Insurance, securities, and bank products were sold by different institutions, and little cross-market competition existed.

During the past thirty years, changes in size and technology have opened financial markets to buyers and sellers around the globe, transaction times are now measured in fractions of a second, and consumers have been given access to a broad range of valuable products from a single provider. Innovations in products and technology, and the global nature of financial markets are here to stay. An unnecessarily fragmented and outdated regulatory system imposes costs in several ways: inefficiencies in operation, limitations on innovation, and competition restraints that are difficult to justify.

2.1. Consolidate federal financial services regulation

The benefits of a more unified federal approach to financial services regulation have been a constant theme in proposals for regulatory reform, some of which were under consideration and announced before the onset of the current financial crisis. For example, the Group of 30, in its very first recommendation, called for "government-insured deposit taking institutions" to be subject to "prudential regulation and supervision by a single regulator."[176] The Committee on Capital Markets Regulation has similarly called for a consolidated U.S. Financial Services Authority (USFSA) that "would regulate all aspects of the financial system including market structure and activities and safety and soundness."[177] Treasury's Blueprint for a Modernized Financial Regulatory Structure recommends a Prudential Financial Regulatory Agency (PFRA) with oversight over "financial institutions with some type of explicit government guarantee associated with their business operations."[178]

The current regulatory structure for oversight of federally chartered depository institutions is highly fragmented, with supervision spread among at least five agencies including the OCC, OTS, FDIC, National Credit Union Administration (NCUA), and the Federal Reserve. Thus, Congress should streamline oversight of these federally chartered and insured institutions.

2.2. Modernize the federal charter for insured depository institutions

There are many kinds of insured depositories operating under unique charters including national banks, thrifts, state chartered members of the Federal Reserve system, state chartered nonmembers, credit card banks, federal and state credit unions, and state charted industrial loan corporations. While this vast array of institution type may have had a sound historical basis, changes in the national economy and regulatory landscape have made many of these differences functionally obsolete. Although regulatory competition can prove beneficial, the current state of duplicative banking regulation has several negative consequences as well, including unnecessary consumption of federal regulatory resources, consumer transparency, and differences in charters for largely similar institutions, which can lead to unfair competitive advantages for institutions governed by certain charters over others.

In particular, the OCC and the OTS play a very similar role for two classes of depository institutions which were once were quite different in nature, but now compete for the same customers, offering similar services. The thrift charter was originally instituted to foster the creation of financial services organizations to encourage home ownership by ensuring a wide availability of home mortgage loans. Due to a number of national policy changes that have been instituted over the last several decades to encourage homeownership and the decreasing share thrifts have of the residential mortgage market in relation to commercial banks, a unique thrift charter is no longer necessary to meet this goal. Moreover, the constraints of the thrift charter limit the diversification of thrifts' loan portfolios, which only exacerbates their ability to remain financially healthy in a weak real estate market.

Many individuals and organizations reviewing the current regulatory landscape have come to the conclusion that these agencies, and their corresponding federal thrift, and federal bank charters should be unified. In fact, back in 1994, former Federal Reserve Governor, John P. LaWare recommended combining the OCC with the OTS.[179] Similarly, in 1996, the GAO recommended that primary supervisory responsibilities of the OTS, OCC, and the FDIC be consolidated into a new, independent Federal Banking Commission.[180]

Congress should consider other steps to modernize and rationalize the federal charter system. Each class of charter should be reviewed for purpose, structure, cost and distinct characteristics. Unnecessary differences are potential sources of confusion, conflict, or taxpayer risk, and should be eliminated wherever possible.

2.3. Consolidate the SEC and CFTC

Similar to the rationalization that is needed in banking regulation, consolidation of securities regulation in the U.S. through the merger of the SEC and the CFTC should also be undertaken. Most countries have vested the power to oversee all securities markets in one agency, and for good reason—more efficient, consistent regulation that protects consumers in a more uniform manner.

As the Treasury Blueprint states: "Product and market participant convergence, market linkages, and globalization have rendered regulatory bifurcation of the futures and securities markets untenable, potentially harmful, and inefficient. The realities of the current marketplace have significantly diminished, if not entirely eliminated, the original rationale for the regulatory bifurcation between futures and securities markets."[181]

It further notes that: "Jurisdictional disputes have ensued as the increasing complexity and hybridization of financial products have made 'definitional' determination of agency jurisdiction (i.e., whether a product is appropriately regulated as a security under the federal securities laws or as a futures contract under the CEA) increasingly problematic. This ambiguity has spawned a history of jurisdictional disputes, which critics claim have hindered innovation, limited investor choice, harmed investor protection, and encouraged product innovators and their consumers to seek out other, more integrated international markets, engage in regulatory arbitrage, or evade regulatory oversight altogether."[182]

In testimony before this panel, Joel Seligman, President of the University of Rochester and a leading authority on securities law, agreed, stating, a "pivotal criterion to addressing the right balance in designing a regulatory system is one that reduces as much as is feasible regulatory arbitrage. Whatever the historical reasons for the existence of a separate SEC and CFTC, the costs of having a system where in borderline cases those subject to regulation may choose their regulator is difficult to justify."[183]

The most significant obstacle to this proposal is a political one. Congressional oversight of the two agencies is split between two committees in both the House and Senate. Consolidation would most likely mean that one committee would lose out, leading to a classic turf war. Since the nature of futures trading has evolved significantly over the years, and is now dominated by non-agricultural products, the Senate Banking and House Financial Services Committees would be the appropriate venue for all congressional securities oversight.

2.4. Establish an optional federal charter for national insurance firms

The U.S. federal financial service regulatory infrastructure contains no agency or organization responsible for oversight of national insurance firms. As far back as 1871, regulators saw the need for uniform national standards for insurance. That year, former New York Insurance Commissioner, George W. Miller, who founded the National Association of Insurance Commissioners (NAIC), made the following statement: "The Commissioners are now fully prepared to go before their various legislative committees with recommendations for a system of insurance law which shall be the same in all States, not reciprocal but identical, not retaliatory, but uniform."[184] That need for uniform standards has grown quite considerably during the past 138 years.

Congress should institute a federal charter that may be utilized by insurance firms to underwrite, market, and sell products on a national basis. While individual state insurance regulators have effectively managed state guarantee pools, as well as safety and soundness within their jurisdiction, they simply are not equipped to effectively oversee a global firm such as AIG, which had 209 subsidiaries at the time the federal government acted to prevent its collapse in the fall of 2008. Of the 209 subsidiaries, only twelve fell under the jurisdiction of the New York insurance commissioner, which was effectively AIG's primary regulator.[185]

By allowing insurance firms to choose between a unified national charter or maintaining operations under existing state regulation, Congress can build upon the success of state guarantee pools and maintain state jurisdiction over premium taxes. A national charter would also allow regulators to take a comprehensive view of the safety and soundness of large insurance companies and to better understand the potential risks they may pose to the strength of the broader U.S. economy. Lastly, a federal insurance regulator would be able to implement effective consumer protection, provide a clear federal voice to coordinate global insurance regulation with foreign counterparts, and ensure appropriate access for U.S. insurance companies in overseas markets.

3. Strengthening Capital Requirements and Improving Risk Management

The experience of the past two years demonstrates that our financial system was far more susceptible to shocks from the housing sector than it should have been, as a result of capital requirements that were insufficient to sustain financial institutions in time of stress. Those weaknesses were in turn further exacerbated by certain standards and practices, such as a heavy reliance on credit rating agencies and the application of mark-to-market accounting standards. To ensure that our financial system can better withstand these kinds of shocks, capital requirements should be strengthened and risk management should be enhanced.

3.1. Strengthen capital requirements for financial institutions

One of the key lessons that has emerged from this crisis is that our financial institutions did not have adequate capital reserves to weather the turmoil in the housing market due in large part to the fact that many of the assets they held were inextricably linked to this market. One way to address this problem would be to ensure that regulators can demand that financial institutions increase their capital during flush times. Those reserves could then serve as a cushion during bad times when capital is much harder to raise. The provisioning requirements would be based on the health of the economy as a whole, thus building upon systemic strength and buffering against systemic weakness.

These countercyclical requirements would be quite different from those governing the regulatory capital that financial institutions are required to hold today. The current capital rules for lending are out of date, subject to manipulation, and do not accurately reflect the risks associated with lending activities. That said, there are also significant flaws and risks associated with the new capital rules called for by the Basel II regime.

Much of the initial modeling now available suggests that average capital requirements for banks subject to Basel II methodologies would decrease. The determination to allow the largest and most complex banks to use internally developed, historical models for the purpose of determining capital risk charges merits further and closer scrutiny. Given the current financial crisis and the federal guaranty on deposits that banks enjoy, weak capital requirements called for by Basel II could leave taxpayers on the hook yet again.

3.2. End conduits and off-balance-sheet accounting for bank assets

Apart from its procyclicality, Basel II permitted banks and other financial institutions to keep assets such as mortgage-backed securities off their books in conduits or structured investment vehicles on the grounds that these assets were high-quality and low-risk. Even if such an assessment were accurate—and the past two years have demonstrated that it was not—off-balance-sheet arrangements such as this permit financial institutions to game the regulatory requirements in place. These off-balance-sheet arrangements were made even more dangerous by the perception that their liabilities were implicitly guaranteed by the institutions that sponsored them, which permitted even greater leverage to build before the credit crisis hit. Thus, all assets and liabilities of a financial institution should be held on the balance sheet. If nothing else, one of the lessons of this credit crisis is the necessary steps should be taken to eliminate the notion of an "implicit guarantee" of anything in our markets.

3.3. Adjust the application of mark-to-market accounting rules

Fair value accounting should be revised and reformed. As things stand now, the accounting rules magnify economic stress and can have serious procyclical effects. When markets turn sour or panic, assets in a mark-to-market accounting system must be repeatedly written down, causing financial institutions to appear weaker than they might otherwise be. A superior accounting system would not require financial institutions to write down their assets at a time when prices have fallen precipitously during a rapid downturn as in the collapse of a bubble. Thus, alternative asset valuation procedures—such as discounted cash flow—should be used, and it should be made easier for financial institutions to declare assets as held-to-maturity during these periods. In normal markets, prices will fluctuate within a limited range, and will rise slowly if at all. But in times of crisis—such as the one we are facing—write-downs beget fire sales, which beget further writedowns.

In late September 2008, the SEC released guidelines that allowed companies greater flexibility in valuing assets in a nonfunctioning market. Such changes are encouraging. Moving forward, accounting rules have to provide transparency and the most accurate depiction of economic reality as possible. It is for the best that the development of accounting rules should not be conducted in the political arena. However, it is clear that the rules need to be improved, taking into account the lessons learned from recent events. Ultimately, greater transparency and accuracy in accounting standards are necessary to restore investor confidence.

3.4. Eliminate the credit rating agencies' cartel

The failure of the credit rating agencies in the financial crisis could not be more apparent. Much like the GSEs, the credit rating agencies benefited from a unique status conferred upon them by the government. They operated as an effective oligopoly to earn above-market returns while being spared market discipline in instances where their ratings turned out to be inaccurate. The special status of the rating agencies should be ended so as to open the ratings field to competition from new entrants and to encourage investors and other users of ratings not to rely upon a ratings label as a substitute for due diligence.

3.5. Establishing a clearinghouse for credit default swaps

Despite recent criticism heaped upon them, the thriving credit default swaps (CDS) market demonstrates the valuable role that innovation plays in improving the functioning of our financial markets. Through the use of CDS, investors and lenders can hedge their credit exposures more efficiently, thereby freeing up additional credit capacity, which has in turn enabled banks to expand credit facilities and reduce costs of funds for borrowers. CDS have enabled asset managers and other institutional investors to adjust their credit exposures quickly and at a lower cost than alternative investment instruments, and have enabled market participants to better assess and manage their credit. CDS have also enabled market participants to value illiquid assets for which market quotations might not be readily available.

Despite their many benefits and the crucial role that CDS have come to play in the financial system in managing risk, legitimate concerns have arisen regarding the transparency of the system and the management of counterparty risk. To address these concerns, the Federal Reserve, the CFTC, and the SEC have recently agreed on general principles to provide consistent oversight of one or more clearinghouses for CDS trades. The proposed guidelines will result in more public information on potential risks being provided to counterparties and investors, as well as the mitigation of any systemic losses caused by potential fallout from the CDS market.

These principles constitute a valuable first step in creating a CDS clearinghouse and will further improve a product that has thus far proven invaluable in managing risk when prudently used. A properly structured clearinghouse, capitalized by its members, spreads the risk of default and fosters market stability by acting as the sole counterparty to each buyer and seller. A clearinghouse will allow performance risk to be isolated to net exposure, rather than related to the much larger gross positions in the market.

A number of reforms have already reduced risk in the CDS market. The CDS market has already dramatically increased margin, mark-to-market and collateral requirements for hedge funds and other investment institutions on the other side of any trade. And at the behest of the New York Federal Reserve and other regulators, record keeping has improved; trade confirmations, for example, now must be tendered quickly. Buyers of CDS protection now also must formally approve any switch of their coverage from one insurer to another. Previously, the insured might not know who was its latest counterparty.

A clearinghouse, however, may not be appropriate for the most complex and unique over-the- counter derivatives. Moreover, because a clearinghouse arrangement spreads risk to other market participants, it could encourage excessive risk taking by some, especially if risks associated with more exotic products are not priced properly due to information asymmetry. Policy makers and regulators should continue to work with the private sector to facilitate a CDS clearinghouse that provides greater transparency and reduces systemic risk in the broader financial markets.

4. Address Systemic Risk

4.1. Consolidate the work of the president's working group and the financial stability oversight board to create a cross-agency panel for identifying and monitoring systemic risk

Systemic risk can materialize in a broad range of areas within our financial system: at both depository and nondepository institutions, within either consumer or commercial markets, as a result of poor fiscal or monetary policy, or initiated by domestic or global activity. Thus, it is impractical, and perhaps a dangerous concentration of power, to give one single regulator the power to set or modify any and all standards relating to such risk. Systemic risk oversight and management must be a collaborative effort, bringing together the leading authorities for addressing safety and soundness, managing economic policy, and ensuring consumer protection.

One alternative to a single systemic risk regulator would be to develop a panel of federal agencies to consider jointly these important questions. The Presidential Working Group (PWG) was established after the stock market crash of 1987 to make recommendations for enhancing market integrity and investor confidence. Similarly, the Financial Stability Oversight Board (F SOB) was established under the EESA in 2008 as a cross-agency group to oversee the Troubled Assets Relief Program (TARP) and evaluate the ways in which funds might be used to enhance market stability. Both groups include the Treasury, the Federal Reserve, and the SEC. The PWG adds the CFTC, while the FSOB includes the Housing Secretary and the Director of the Federal Housing Finance Agency (FHFA), which oversees the housing GSEs.

While the quarterly evaluation of TARP operations provided by the FSOB will continue through the life of the program, the broad mission and structure of these two organizations are, in many respects, redundant. Moreover, they represent the collaborative, cross-agency structure that would best provide insight in to the practices, policies, and trends that might contribute to systemic risk within the financial system.

By combining and refocusing the efforts of these two organizations, Congress can establish a body with the requisite tools to identify, monitor, and evaluate systemic risk. The panel can make specific legislative recommendations, as well as encourage immediate action consistent with the significant regulatory powers already vested in its members.

A Panel comprised of the Federal Reserve, the Treasury, the primary regulator of federally insured depository institutions, and the combined SEC/CFTC, would have authority to access detailed financial information from regulated financial institutions, require disclosure of information necessary to evaluate risk, and require that financial institutions to undertake corrective actions to address systemic weakness.

Disagreement with Panel Regulatory Recommendations

In far too many areas, the Panel Report offers recommendations or policy options that are rife with moral hazard and the potential for unintended consequences. Given that some of the principal causes of this financial crisis include the moral hazard embedded in the charter of Fannie Mae and Freddie Mac, market-distorting housing mandates like the CRA, and the unintended consequences of a credit rating agency certification process which restricted competition, we must be particularly mindful of these risks. In some cases, a highlighted action may appear benign, but the more detailed summary includes proposals or policy "options" that cannot be supported.

Other sections, such as those dealing with systemic risk and leverage, include highly proscriptive proposals that would be difficult, if not impossible to implement outside the walls of academia. Finally, the Panel Report all but ignores the critical role played by the Federal Reserve's highly accommodative monetary policy, and the host of troubles created by the government charter and implicit backing of the GSEs. Avoiding discussion of such important components of the crisis will inevitably lead one to set the wrong priorities for reform. While not exhaustive, the following represents a list of the more significant disagreements held with the Panel Recommendations for Improvement:

1. The Panel Report calls for a "body to identify and regulate institutions with systemic significance" and "[i]mpose heightened regulatory requirements for systemically significant institutions." The

recommendations suggest that firms designated as such are to be subjected to unique capital and liquidity requirements, as well as special fees for insurance. Although it is important that regulators work to identify, monitor, and address systemic risk, such explicit actions are more likely to have unintended and severe negative consequences.

Publicly identifying "systemically significant institutions" will create significant moral hazard, the cost of which will far outweigh any potential regulatory benefits. Consider the two possible effects of being identified as such. First, in one case, the cost and burdens of additional capital and regulatory requirements (as recommended) place a firm at a competitive disadvantage relative to its peers. Thus, the competitive strength of a systemically significant firm is impaired, raising the probability of a business failure—an undesirable outcome.

In the alternative case, the market may view designation as a *de facto* guarantee of public support in during times of financial stress. The firm attains a beneficial market status, and enjoys advantages such as a lower cost of capital in the public markets. The costs of failure are thus socialized, while profits remain in private hands (much as was the case for the GSEs, Fannie Mae and Freddie Mac). Recent events make clear that this scenario is perhaps an even more undesirable outcome than the former.

Unfortunately, these are the only two practical outcomes of any designation—either markets will view it as a competitive burden or as a competitive advantage. It is unrealistic to argue that such a "significant" designation would be viewed as competitively neutral. Moreover, it is unreasonable to assume that government will manage the potential moral hazard more effectively than was done in the case of the GSEs.

2. The Panel Report recommends the formation of "a single federal regulator for consumer credit products." Such an action would isolate the activity of creating and enforcing consumer protection standards from oversight of safety and soundness in financial institutions.

   The regulation of any federal financial firm requires the balancing of multiple policy choices and should be done by one institution. Experience has shown us with the GSE model that having two stated goals, one for safety and soundness and one for social policy, inherently will lead to conflict. Since the new consumer product regulator would be able to affect all financial institutions, eventually those rules will conflict with a bank's profitability, capital levels, and ultimately, solvency. Under this Panel proposal, an independent agency would have power to impose regulations that could well undermine the health of banks, but would not be responsible for the safety and soundness of those banks.

This balance is of particular significance within institutions that have been provided with explicit taxpayer funded guarantees, such as FDIC insurance. By placing both responsibilities with the same regulator, greater assurance is provided that taxpayer interests will not be placed in jeopardy by regulations that unnecessarily weaken capital or competitive position.

3. The Panel Report broadly calls for the adoption of new regulations to "to curtail leverage." While the recommendation implies that regulators across the spectrum of financial institutions set inappropriate standards for leverage, this simply is not the case.

Few, if any, observers of the current crisis have argued that capital standards set by the FDIC and other federal and state banking regulators overseeing depository institutions were set at dangerously low levels. To the extent that FDIC insured institutions have become troubled, it has been largely the results of deteriorating loan quality. Thousands of such institutions across the country remain strong and healthy. Raising their capital standards now in an effort to "curtail leverage" would be highly procyclical and would sharply limit the availability of credit for consumers and businesses.

Without question, there were some financial firms, notably non-depository institutions such as broker-dealers, that were allowed to raise their leverage ratios substantially in recent years. The SEC ruling issued in 2004, which allowed alternative net capital requirements for broker-dealers, contributed significantly to the failures of both Bear Sterns and Lehman Brothers. The regulatory decision to rely on internal models for risk weighting assets appears, in retrospect, to have been a major miscalculation.

Moreover, prudent regulators may wish to consider adopting capital policies that are more counter- cyclical as well, to encourage the building of stronger reserves during good times and ensure greater stability in periods of financial stress. Blanket mandates to "curtail leverage," however, will only restrict access to credit and limit successful lending models where they are needed most.

4. The Panel Report argues that: "Hedge funds and private equity funds are money managers and should be regulated according to the same principles that govern the regulation of money managers generally." The recommendation fails to recognize the important distinctions between investment firms and fails to explain why these distinctions should be ignored.

   There exist clear and dramatic differences between managing capital allocation on behalf of a $5 billion dollar pension fund, and investing funds placed in a personal IRA or 40 1k. Under current law, private equity, venture capital, and hedge funds may not be marketed to retail investors. While they remain subject to all regulations regarding trading and exchange rules and regulations, they are not subject to the marketing and registration requirements designed to protect smaller, unsophisticated investors, because they do not serve that market.

   Suggesting that more regulation should be imposed on these entities in light of the current crisis ignores the fact that even under the tremendous financial upheaval of the past year, no major hedge funds have declared bankruptcy, and taxpayers have been exposed to no losses resulting from failed hedge fund or private equity investment activity.

   Finally, it may be worth noting that several high-profile hedge fund management firms were among the first to publicly and accurately assess the dangers inherent in the housing finance system, mortgage backed securities, and Fannie Mae and Freddie Mac.

5. The Panel Report call for Congress to "[e]liminate federal pre-emption of application of state consumer protection laws to national banks." Such a change would effectively defeat the purpose of a uniform federal charter for insured depository institutions.

   As previously mentioned, the regulation of any federal financial firm requires the balancing of multiple policy choices and should be done by one institution. By giving state regulators the power to affect bank profitability, capital levels, and solvency standards, this proposal would greatly enhance risk and curtail innovation in our system. Under the Panel proposal, states would not be responsible for the safety and soundness of federally chartered banks, but would have authority to impose regulations that could well undermine the health of those banks.

   Allowing states to impose their own consumer protection laws also undermines the fundamental purpose of a federal banking charter.

Congress established federal financial charters to enable firms to offer products and services on a uniform national basis. Standardization of products and services lowers costs, and acts as an incentive for innovation by enabling new products to be brought to market sooner. Allowing every state to impose its own set of product or business standards on national banks would represent a step backwards, away from strong well-balanced federal regulation that allows national firms to compete effectively with global peers.

6. The Panel Report calls for new "tax incentives to encourage long–term-oriented pay packages," which would represent an unprecedented intervention in the operation of private employment markets.

   The Federal Government should not structure the tax code to reward, penalize or manipulate compensation. Congress attempted to do this in the Omnibus Reconciliation Act of 1993, Pub..L. No. 103-66, which contained the so-called "Million-Dollar Pay Cap."[186] It not only failed to achieve the stated goals of its authors, it had unintended consequences: by raising taxes on cash compensation, more firms chose to compensate executives with large packages of stock options, resulting in numerous high-profile multimillion-dollar "pay days" when the options were exercised.

   Compensation committees should establish executive pay policies that are fair, encourage sound long-term decisions, and are fully disclosed to shareholders and the public. Using the tax code to design an ideal pay structure will certainly have unintended negative consequences, as has been demonstrated by past action, nor will it be successful in deterring companies from paying their employees what they wish to attract and retain the best available talent.

7. The Panel Report calls upon Congress to "consider creating a Credit Rating Review Board" which would be given the sole power to approve ratings required by pension fund managers and others to purchase investment securities.

APPENDIX: OTHER REPORTS ON FINANCIAL REGULATORY REFORM

Other reports on financial regulatory reform that are comparable to this chapter in various respects are itemized in the following list and then briefly summarized in the table below. Reports in both list and table appear in reverse chronological order by the name of the issuing organization. In the list, each item is followed by a short-form reference in brackets.

Group of 30 (G-30). *Financial Reform: A Framework for Financial Stability*. January 15, 2009. http://www.group30.org/pubs/pub_1460.htm. [G-30 January 2009]

Committee on Capital Markets Regulation. *Recommendations for Reorganizing the U.S. Financial Regulatory Structure*. January 14, 2009. *http://www.capmktsreg.org/.* [CCMR January 2009]

Robert Kuttner, Prepared for Dēmos. *Financial Regulation After the Fall*. January, 2009. http://www.demos.org/pubs/reg_fall_1_8_09%20(2).pdf). [Kuttner/Dēmos January 2009]

United States Government Accountability Office (GAO). *Financial Regulation: A Framework for Crafting and Assessing Proposals to Modernize the Outdated U.S. Financial Regulatory System.* (GAO-09-216). January, 2009. http://www.gao.gov/new.items/d09216.pdf. [GAO January 2009]

North American Securities Administrators Association. *Proceedings of the NASAA Financial Services Regulatory Reform Roundtable*. December 11, 2008.http://www.nasaa.org/content/Files/Proceedings_NASAA_Regulatory_Reform_Roundtable.pdf. [NASAA December 2008]

President's Working Group On Financial Markets (PWG). *Progress Update on March Policy Statement on Financial Market Developments*. October, 2008. http://www.ustreas.gov/press [PWG October 2008]

Group of 30 (G-30). *The Structure of Financial Supervision: Approaches and Challenges in a Global Marketplace*. October, 2008. *http://www.group30.org/pubs/pub_1428.htm.* [G-30 October 2008]

Financial Stability Forum (FSF). *Report of the Financial Stability Forum on Enhancing Market and Institutional Resilience and the Follow-Up on*

Implementation. April 7, 2008 and October 10, 2008. http://www. fsforum. org/about/overview.htm.
[FSF April 2008 and October 2008]

Basel Committee on Banking Supervision. *Principles for Sound Liquidity Risk Management and Supervision*. September, 2008. http://www. bis.org/ publ/bcbs144.htm.
[Basel Liquidity Risk Management September 2008]

Professor Lawrence A. Cunningham, for Council of Institutional Investors. *Some Investor Perspectives on Financial Regulation Proposals*. Sept., 2008. *http://www.cii.org/UserFiles/file/Sept2008Market Regulation.pdf.*
[Cunningham/CII September 2008]

The Counterparty Risk Management Policy Group (CRMPG) III. *Containing Systemic Risk: The Road to Reform*. August 6, 2008. *http://www. crmpolicygroup.org/docs/CRMPG-III.pdf.*
[CRMPG III August 2008]

Institute of International Finance (IIF). *Final Report of the IIF Committee on Market Best Practices: Principles of Conduct and Best Practice Recommendations—Financial Services Industry Response to the Market Turmoil of 2007–2008*. July, 2008. *http://www. ieco.clarin.com/ 2008/07/ 17/iff.pdf.*
[IIF July 2008]

Securities Industry and Financial Markets Association (SIFMA). *Recommendations of the Securities Industry and Financial Markets Association Credit Rating Agency Task Force*. July 2008. *http://www. sifma.org/capital_markets*
[SIFMA July 2008]

United States Securities and Exchange Commission Staff. *Summary Report of Issues Identified in the Commission Staff's Examination of Select Credit Rating Agencies*. July, 2008. http://www.sec.gov/ news/studies/ 2008/ craexamination070808.pdf.
[SEC Staff July 2008]

International Organization of Securities Commissions Technical Committee (IOSCO). *Report On the Subprime Crisis*. May, 2008. *http://www.iosco. org/library/pubdocs/pdf/IOSCOPD273.pdf.* [IOSCO Subprime Crisis May 2008]

International Organization of Securities Commissions Technical Committee (IOSCO). *The Role of Credit Rating in Structured Finance Markets*. May, 2008. *http://www.iosco.org/library/pubdocs/pdf/IOS COPD270.pdf.*
[IOSCO CRA May 2008]

President's Working Group on Financial Markets (PWG). *Policy Statement on Financial Market Developments*. March, 2008. *http://www.ustreas.gov/press* [PWG March 2008]

Senior Supervisors Group (SSG). *Observations on Risk Management Practices in the Recent Market Turbulence*. March 6, 2008. http://www.newyorkfed.org/newsevents/news/banking. [SSG March 2008]

United States Department of the Treasury. *Blueprint for a Modernized Financial Regulatory Structure*. March, 2008. *http://www.treas.gov/ press*. [Treasury March 2008]

Financial Services Roundtable (FSR). *The Blueprint for U.S. Financial Competitiveness*. Nov. 2007, http://www.fsround.org/cec/blueprint.htm. [FSF April 2007 and October 2007]

United States Chamber of Commerce Commission on the Regulation of U.S. Capital Markets in the 21st Century. *Report and Recommendations of the Commission on the Regulation of U.S. Capital Markets in the 21st Century*. March 2007. *http://www. uschamber. com/publications/ reports/ 0703capmarketscomm.htm.*
[Chamber of Commerce March 2007]

Mayor Michael Bloomberg and Senator Charles Schumer, with McKinsey & Company and New York City Economic Development Corporation. *Sustaining New York's and the US' Global Financial Services Leadership.* January, 2007. http://schumer.senate FINAL.pdf.
[Bloomberg/Schumer January 2007]

Committee on Capital Markets Regulation (CCMR). *Interim Report of the Committee on Capital Markets Regulation*. November, 2006. *http:// www. capmktsreg.org/.*[CCMR November 2006]

Name of Issuer	Group of 30 (G-30)
Name of Report	*Financial Reform: A Framework for Financial Stability*
Date of Report	January 15, 2009
Background of Issuer	"The Group of Thirty, established in 1978, is a private, nonprofit, international body composed of very senior representatives of the private and public sectors and academia. It aims to deepen understanding of international economic and financial issues, to explore the international repercussions of decisions taken in the public and private sectors, and to examine the choices available to market practitioners and policymakers." http://www.group30.org/

Objectives of the Report
The report considers how the financial system should be organized after the present crisis. It seeks a consensus on future arrangements that will be useful both in the long term and in restoring confidence in the present. The report examines the policy issues related to redefining the scope and boundaries of prudential regulation; the structure of prudential regulation, including the role of central banks, the implications for the workings of "lender- of-last-resort" facilities and other elements of the official "safety net," and the need for greater international coordination; improvements in governance, risk management, regulatory policies, and accounting practices and standards; and improvements in transparency and financial infrastructure arrangements.

Name of Issuer	Committee on Capital Markets Regulation.
Name of Report	Recommendations for Reorganizing the U.S. Financial Regulatory Structure
Date of Report	January 14, 2009
Background of Issuer	The Committee on Capital Markets Regulation is a not-for-profit research organization addressing issues in United States capital markets. Its membership, focus, and activities are described at http://www.capmktsreg.org/index.html.

Objectives of the Report
Its 2009 report recommends "sweeping" changes in regulatory organization. The report focuses on the federal regulatory structure, not discussing—but stating the potential for commentary in a future report—on the role or states or self-regulatory organizations, internal agency organization, and global coordination.

Name of Issuer	Robert Kuttner, prepared for ' PRV_
Name of Report	*Financial Regulation After the Fall*
Date of Report	January 9, 2009
Background of Issuer	Robert Kuttner, founder and co-editor of *The American Prospect*, prepared this paper for ' PRV . ' PRV_ is a non-partisan public policy research and advocacy organization headquartered in New York City.

Objectives of the Report
Kuttner writes that "This paper is an effort to catalogue abuses and suggest ways to think about regulatory remedies. Because of the continuing undertow of the market- fundamentalist ideology and the continuing political power of the very people and institutions that brought us this catastrophe, some of the most robust remedies will seem at the margins of mainstream debate. But, in order to move them to center stage where they can gain a proper hearing, it is necessary to at least inject these ideas into discussion."

Name of Issuer	United States Government Accountability Office (GAO)
Name of Report	*Financial Regulation: A Framework for Crafting and Assessing*
	Proposals to Modernize the Outdated U.S. Financial Regulatory System (GAO-09-216)
Date of Report	January, 2009
Background of Issuer	The United States Government Accountability Office (GAO) is an independent, nonpartisan agency that works for Congress. Its work is done at the request of congressional committees or subcommittees or is mandated by public laws or committee reports, and the GAO also undertakes research under the authority of the Comptroller General. http://www.gao.gov/about/index.html

Objectives of the Report
The Government Accountability Office report describes the origins of the current financial regulatory system, market developments and changes shaping the regulatory systems, and suggests issues to be addressed in designing and evaluating proposals for change. It describes structural gaps and stresses in the system rather than evaluates agencies' implementations of regulatory programs.

Name of Issuer	North American Securities Administrators Association
Name of Report	*Proceedings of the NASAA Financial Services Regulatory Reform Roundtable, December 11, 2008*
Date of Report	December 11, 2008 Organized in 1919, the North American Securities Administrators
Background of Issuer	Organized in 1919, the North American Securities Administrators Association (NASAA) is the oldest international organization devoted to investor protection. NASAA is a voluntary association with a membership consisting of securities administrators in the fifty states, the District of Columbia, Puerto Rico, the U.S. Virgin Islands, Canada, and Mexico http://www. nasaa.org/ home/index.cfm

Objectives of the Report
This document summarizes statements by state securities regulators in a discussion of regulatory reform designed to provide advice to the incoming administration of President Obama. The report stems from the NASAA's core principles for regulatory reform, found at http://www.nasaa.org/issues___answers/legislative_activity/9775.cfm.

Name of Issuer	President's Working Group On Financial Markets (PWG)
Name of Report	*Policy Statement on Financial Market Developments and Progress Update on March Policy Statement on Financial Market Developments*
Date of Report	March, 2008 and October, 2008
Background of Issuer	The President's Working Group on Financial Markets (PWG) consists of the Department of the Treasury, the Federal Reserve, Securities and Exchange Commission, and the Commodity Futures Trading Commission. The Treasury Secretary chairs the group. The PWG worked with the Office of the Comptroller of the Currency and Federal Reserve Bank of New York in preparing these reports.

Objectives of the Report
These policy statements offered recommendations to improve the future state of U.S. and global financial markets. The March statement addressed the causes of the market crisis and offered proposals to mitigate systemic risk, restore investor confidence, and facilitate stable economic growth. The October statement reviewed interim developments and provided a progress report on these initiatives.

Name of Issuer	**Group of 30 (G-30)**
Name of Report	The Structure of Financial Supervision: Approaches and Challenges in a Global Marketplace
Date of Report	October, 2008
Background of Issuer	"The Group of Thirty, established in 1978, is a private, nonprofit, international body composed of very senior representatives of the private and public sectors and academia. It aims to deepen understanding of international economic and financial issues, to explore the international repercussions of decisions taken in the public and private sectors, and to examine the choices available to market practitioners and policymakers." http://www.group30.org/

Objectives of the Report
In July 2007, the Group of 30 (G-30) commenced a seventeen-jurisdiction review of financial regulatory approaches. The G-30 Report outlines four approaches to financial supervision in use in jurisdictions around the world and assesses the strengths and weaknesses of each approach. Work on the October 2008 Report began before the current crisis, and thus it does not assess how different regulatory regimes performed in response to the crisis.

Name of Issuer	**Financial Stability Forum (FSF)**
Name of Report	Report of the Financial Stability Forum on Enhancing Market and Institutional Resilience and the Follow-Up on Implementation
Date of Report	April 7, 2008 and October 10, 2008
Background of Issuer	The Financial Stability Forum (FSF), first convened in 1999, consists of senior representatives of national financial authorities, international financial institutions, international regulatory and supervisory groupings, committees of central bank experts and the European Central Bank. The FSF is serviced by a secretariat housed at the Bank for International Settlements. The FSF assesses vulnerabilities in the international financial system, identifies and oversees appropriate responses, and improves coordination and information exchange among the various authorities responsible for financial stability. It seeks to strengthen financial systems and the stability of international financial markets, and any recommended changes are enacted by the relevant national and international financial authorities. http://www.fsforum.org/about/overview.htm

Objectives of the Report
In October 2007, the G7 Ministers and Central Bank Governors asked the Financial Stability Forum to analyze the causes and weaknesses producing the financial crisis and make recommendations by April 2008 to increase the resilience of markets and institutions. Collaborating in the work were the Basel Committee on Banking Supervision (BCSB), the International Organization of Securities Commissions (IOSCO), the International Association of Insurance Supervisors (IAIS), the Joint Forum, the International Accounting Standards Board (IASB), the Committee on Payment and Settlement Systems (CPSS), the Committee on the Global Financial System (CGFS), the International Monetary Fund (IMF), the Bank for International Settlements (BIS) and national authorities in key financial centers. The FSF also drew on private sector participants. The follow-up report in October reviewed the implementation of the recommendations made in the April report.

Name of Issuer	**Basel Committee on Banking Supervision**
Name of Report	*Principles of Sound Liquidity Risk Management and Supervision*
Date of Report	September, 2008
Background of Issuer	The Basel Committee on Banking Supervision provides a forum for regular cooperation on banking supervisory matters. Its objective is to enhance understanding of key supervisory issues and improve the quality of banking supervision worldwide. It seeks to do so by exchanging information on national supervisory issues, approaches and techniques, with a view to promoting common understanding. At times, the committee uses this common understanding to develop guidelines and supervisory standards in areas where they are considered desirable. http://www.bis.org/bcbs/

Objectives of the Report
Citing its review of banks' response to recent market turmoil, the committee faulted banks for failing to pay attention to basic principles of liquidity risk management. The committee found that many banks did not have an adequate framework in place to account for liquidity risks posed by products and business lines, causing incentives to be "misaligned" with overall risk tolerance. In an attempt to "underscore the importance of establishing a robust liquidity risk management framework that is well integrated into the bank-wide risk management process," the report contains principles and related best practices recommendations designed to increase banks' resilience to liquidity stress.

Name of Issuer	**Professor Lawrence A. Cunningham, for Council of Institutional Investors**
Name of Report	*Some Investor Perspectives on Financial Regulation Proposals*
Date of Report	September, 2008
Background of Issuer	The Council of Institutional Investors (CII) is a nonprofit association of public, union, and corporate pension funds with combined assets that exceed $3 trillion. Member funds are major long-term shareowners. Professor Lawrence A. Cunningham, author of the paper, is Henry St. George Tucker III Research Professor of Law at George Washington University Law School.

Objectives of the Report
Professor Lawrence A. Cunningham of George Washington University Law School wrote this paper for the Council of Institutional Investors (CII). It assesses, "from an investor's perspective," mutual recognition in securities regulation, integration of securities and futures regulation, and a model of financial regulation relying on a single agency to oversee all financial markets. The analysis examines the U.S. Department of the *Treasury's Blueprint for a Modernized Financial Regulatory Structure.*

Name of Issuer	**The Counterparty Risk Management Policy Group (CRMPG) III**
Name of Report	*Containing Systemic Risk: The Road to Reform*
Date of Report	August 6, 2008
Background of Issuer	The Counterparty Risk Management Policy Group III is a group of senior officials and staff from a number of major financial institutions. This is the third report prepared by the CRMPG focusing on improving risk management and financial infrastructure, with the earlier reports issued in 1999 and 2005.
Objectives of the Report	
The CRMPG sets out a series of private initiatives intended to complement official oversight to help contain systemic risk. These include reconsideration of accounting standards for consolidation under U.S. GAAP of entities currently off balance sheet coming on balance sheet; measurement and management of high-risk financial instruments; improvements in risk monitoring and management; and measures to strengthen the resiliency of financial markets generally and the credit markets in particular, with a special emphasis on OTC derivatives and credit default swaps. The report also highlights important emerging issues.	

Name of Issuer	Institute of International Finance (IIF)
Name of Report	*Final Report of the IIF Committee on Market Best Practices: Principles of Conduct and Best Practice Recommendations— Financial Services Industry Response to the Market Turmoil of 2007–2008*
Date of Report	July, 2008
Background of Issuer	The Institute of International Finance, established in 1983 in response to the international debt crisis, is a global association of financial institutions. Its members include most of the world's largest commercial and investment banks and a growing number of insurance companies and investment management firms. http://www.iif.com/

Objectives of the Report
The IIF Committee on Market Best Practices set out principles of conduct, best practice recommendations, and considerations for officials. The report examined risk management; compensation policies; liquidity risk; structured vehicles such as conduits and securitization; valuation; credit underwriting, ratings, and investor due diligence in securitization markets; and transparency and disclosure. The committee suggested that rigorous self-assessment and monitoring are necessary to improve conduct in each of these areas. However, higher industry standards can only work within an effective and efficient regulatory framework.

Name of Issuer	Securities Industry and Financial Markets Association (SIFMA)
Name of Report	*Recommendations of the Securities Industry and Financial Markets Association Credit Rating Agency Task Force*
Date of Report	July, 2008
Background of Issuer	The Securities Industry and Financial Markets Association (SIFMA) is a principal trade association of the financial services industry. Its membership consists of securities firms, banks, and asset managers. Its stated mission is to promote policies and practices to expand and improve financial markets, help to create new products and services and create efficiencies for member firms, and preserve and enhance the public's trust and confidence in financial markets and the industry.

Objectives of the Report
The Securities Industry and Financial Markets Association (SIFMA) Credit Rating Agency Task Force is a global task force formed to examine credit ratings and credit rating agencies (CRAs). It includes experts in structured finance, corporate bonds, municipal bonds, and risk and members from the United States, Europe, and Asia. The President's Working Group on Financial Markets (PWG) designated the task force as the private-sector group to provide the PWG with industry recommendations on credit rating matters. The task force identified the credit-rating-related causal variables contributing to the current crisis; ranked, in order of importance designated by its members, sixteen key issues; and addressed those issues in its recommendations.

Name of Issuer	**United States Securities and Exchange Commission Staff**
Name of Report	*Summary Report of Issues Identified in the Commission Staff's Examination of Select Credit Rating Agencies*
Date of Report	July, 2008
Background of Issuer	United States Securities and Exchange Commission exercises regulatory jurisdiction over the credit rating process.

Objectives of the Report
In August 2007, the staff of the Securities and Exchange Commission conducted examinations of three leading credit rating agencies (CRAs) to review their role in market turmoil. The staff focused on the rating agencies' activities with respect to subprime residential mortgage-backed securities (RMBS) and collateralized debt obligations (CDOs) linked to RMBSs. In July 2008, the staff issued its summary report on issued identified by those examinations.

Name of Issuer	**International Organization of Securities Commissions Technical Committee (IOSCO)**
Name of Report	*Report on the Subprime Crisis*
Date of Report	May, 2008
Background of Issuer	The member agencies of the International Organization of Securities Commissions cooperate to develop and maintain high standards of regulation; exchange information on their respective experiences in order to promote the development of domestic markets; seek to establish standards and an effective surveillance of international securities transactions; and provide mutual assistance to promote the integrity of the markets by a rigorous application of the standards and by effective enforcement against offenses.

Objectives of the Report
IOSCO's *May Report on the Subprime Crisis* identified causes of the market crisis and made recommendations to mitigate the current crisis and prevent such breakdowns in the future.

Name of Issuer	International Organization of Securities Commissions Technical Committee (IOSCO)
Name of Report	*The Role of Credit Rating Agencies in Structured Finance Markets*
Date of Report	May, 2008
Background of Issuer	The member agencies of the International Organization of Securities Commissions cooperate to develop and maintain high standards of regulation; exchange information on their respective experiences in order to promote the development of domestic markets; seek to establish standards and effective surveillance of international securities transactions; and provide mutual assistance to promote the integrity of the markets by a rigorous application of the standards and by effective enforcement against offenses.

Objectives of the Report
Because of apparent failures in the credit rating process, the IOSCO Technical Committee asked its Credit Rating Agency Task Force to analyze the role CRAs play in structured finance markets and to recommend changes to the IOSCO CRA Code of Conduct as necessary. The May 2008 Report and related revisions to the IOSCO Code of Conduct for CRAs are the outgrowth of this effort.

Name of Issuer	Senior Supervisors Group (SSG)
Name of Report	*Observations on Risk Management Practices in the Recent Market Turbulence*
Date of Report	March 6, 2008
Background of Issuer	The Senior Supervisors Group is composedof seven international supervisory agencies, including the French Banking Commission, the German Federal Financial Supervisory Authority, the Swiss Federal Banking Commission, the U.K. Financial Services Authority, and, in the United States, the Office ofthe Comptroller of the Currency, the Securities and Exchange Commission, and the Federal Reserve.

Objectives of the Report
In 2007 the Financial Stability Forum, which promotes international financial stability through information exchange and regulatory cooperation, initiated a study of risk management practices by firms preceding and during the financial crisis. The Senior Supervisors Group (SSG) surveyed eleven global banking organizations and securities firms in 2007 regarding their oversight and risk management, meeting with select firms' senior management in November 2007 and industry representatives in February 2008. Based principally on a survey and access to information on the firms' operations, it identified risk management practices differentiating firms' performance in weathering the crisis. Firms varied in how effectively their senior management team, business line risk owners, and control functions worked together to manage risks.

Name of Issuer	**United States Department of the Treasury**
Name of Report	*Blueprint for a Modernized Financial Regulatory Structure*
Date of Report	March, 2008
Background of Issuer	The Department of the Treasury plays a central role in U.S. financial regulatory policy. For example, the Secretary of the Treasurychairs the President's Working Group on Financial Markets (PWG), currently consisting of the Treasury, Federal Reserve, Securities and Exchange Commission, and Commodity Futures Trading Commission.

Objectives of the Report
The Department of the Treasury's Blueprint for a Modernized Financial Regulatory Structure calls for reorganization of the financial regulatory system. The work on the report began before the market downturn, so the Blueprint does not focus on many of the specific problems surfaced by the financial crisis, nor limits itself to proposing "emergency relief" for current economic ills. Rather, the Blueprint focuses on what it describes as regulatory gaps, redundancies and inefficiencies in the U.S. regulatory system and proposes broad reforms to the domestic regulatory regime.

Name of Issuer	**Financial Services Roundtable (FSR)**
Name of Report	*The Blueprint for U.S. Financial Competitiveness*
Date of Report	November, 2007
Background of Issuer	The Financial Services Roundtable is an organization of banking, securities, insurance, and investment organizations.

Objectives of the Report
The FSR Blue Ribbon Commission on Enhancing Competitiveness developed a set of Guiding Principles for what it called a more balanced, consistent, and predictable legal and financial regulatory system; articulated a financial services reform agenda based upon the application of the Guiding Principles to important legal and regulatory issues; and proposed changes in systems of chartering for existing financial services institutions. The Blueprint for U.S. Financial Competitiveness proposed ten policy reforms.

Name of Issuer	**United States Chamber of Commerce Commission on the Regulation of U.S. Capital Markets in the 21st Century (the Commission)**
Name of Report	*Report and Recommendations of the Commission on the Regulation of U.S. Capital Markets in the 21st Century*
Date of Report	March, 2007
Background of Issuer	The Chamber of Commerce indicates that it is "the world's largest business federation, representing 3 million businesses of all sizes, sectors, and regions, as well as state and local chambers and industry associations…. As the voice of business, the chamber's core purpose is to fight for free enterprise before Congress, the White House, regulatoryagencies, the courts, the court of public opinion, and governments around the world." http://www.uschamber.com/about/default.htm

Objectives of the Report
The Commission stated that it "believes that with quick and decisive adjustments in the U.S. legal and regulatory framework, U.S. government regulators and market participants will be better positioned to ensure that U.S. investor and business interests are best served in the global marketplace. To better protect investors and promote capital formation, the Commission is setting forth a series of recommendations that would significantly improve the U.S. position in the global markets. These recommendations can be implemented quickly and without overly burdensome costs."

Name of Issuer	**Mayor Michael Bloomberg and Senator Charles Schumer, with McKinsey & Company and New York City Economic Development Corporation**
Name of Report	Sustaining New York's and the US' Global Financial Services Leadership
Date of Report	January, 2007
Background of Issuer	To obtain a "comprehensive perspective" on the competitiveness of the U.S. financial services sector, with a particular focus on New York's contribution, Senator Schumer and Mayor Michael Bloombergcommissioned McKinsey & Company and the New York City Economic Development Corporation (NYCEDC) to interview business leaders, subject matter experts in regulatory, legal, and accounting professions, and investor, labor, and consumer groups.

Objectives of the Report
In their January 2007 report, New York City Mayor Michael Bloomberg and Senator Charles Schumer considered whether New York and the United States were at risk of ceding leadership in the financial services industry to international competitors. To obtain a "comprehensive perspective" on the competitiveness of the U.S. financial services sector, with a particular focus on New York's contribution, Senator Schumer and Mayor Bloomberg commissioned McKinsey & Company and the New York City Economic Development Corporation (NYCEDC) to interview business leaders, subject matter experts in regulatory, legal, and accounting professions, and investor, labor, and consumer groups.

Name of Issuer	**Committee on Capital Markets Regulation (CCMR)**
Name of Report	*Interim Report of the Committee on Capital Markets Regulation*
Date of Report	November, 2006
Background of Issuer	The Committee on Capital Markets Regulation is a not-for-profit research organization addressing issues in United States capital markets. Its membership, focus, and activities are described at http://www.capmktsreg.org/index.html.

Objectives of the Report
The Interim Report articulated concerns regarding the impact of regulatory policy and private litigation on United States capital markets.

End Notes

* Submitted under Section 125(b)(2) of Title I of the Emergency Economic Stabilization Act of 2008, Pub. L. No. 110-343

[1] *See* Edmund L. Andrews, *Greenspan Concedes Error on Regulation*, New York Times (Oct. 24, 2008). *See also* House Committee on Oversight and Government Reform, Testimony of Alan Greenspan, *The Financial Crisis and the Role of Federal Regulators*, 110th Cong., at 2 (Oct. 23, 2008) (online at oversight

[2] Emergency Economic Stabilization Act of 2008, Pub. L. No. 110-343, at § 125(b)(2).

[3] On the period of relative financial stability ("the great pause"), *see* David Moss, *An Ounce of Prevention: The Power of Sound Risk Management in Stabilizing the American Financial System* (2009). *See also* Federal Deposit Insurance Corporation, *History of the Eighties—Lessons for the Future, Volume I: An Examination of the Banking Crises of the 1980s and Early 1990s*, at 187 (online at www.fdic.gov/bank/historical/history/167_188.pdf).

[4] *See* Andrea Young, *What Economic Historians Think About the Meltdown*, History News Network (Oct. 20, 2008) (online at hnn.us/articles/55851.html).

[5] In fact, because of the salutary effects of existing regulations, not all failures of financial institutions create the same level of damage. For instance, the government has insured consumer deposits in financial institutions since the New Deal in recognition of the dangers of a loss of depositor confidence. Consequently, it is no longer the risk of shareholder losses that cause fear of systemic crisis, but rather the risk of financial institutions defaulting on fixed obligations.

[6] These mortgages included so-called 2-28s (which were scheduled to reset to a sharply higher interest rate after two years) and option-arms (which allowed customers essentially to set their own payments in an initial period, followed by ballooning payments after that). Whether or not borrowers could reasonably be expected to repay—based on their earning capacity—was no longer always a decisive criterion for lending, particularly against the backdrop of rising home prices. Said one broker of an elderly client who had lost his home as a result of an unaffordable loan, "It's clear he was living beyond his means, and he might not be able to afford this loan. But legally, we don't have a responsibility to tell him this probably isn't going to work out. It's not our obligation to tell them how they should live their lives." *See* Charles Duhigg, *When Shielding Money Clashes with Elders' Free Will*, New York Times (Dec 24, 2007).

[7] Credit card and automobile loans are also securitized and sold in various formats. It remains to be seen whether an increased rate of default on those loans (which can be expected as the economic slowdown deepens) will generate a second wave of severe capital market disruptions.

[8] *See* section III.2.

[9] On the government's role as a risk manager, *see* David Moss, *When All Else Fails: Government as the Ultimate Risk Manager* (2002).

[10] In fact, significant bank failures did not reappear until after the start of bank deregulation in the early 1 980s. Bank deregulation is often said to have started with the Depository Institutions Deregulation and Monetary Control Act of 1980, Pub. L. No. 96-221, and the Depository Institutions Act of 1982, Pub. L. No. 97-320.

[11] Modern economic research has shown that markets can only function efficiently—that Adam Smith's "invisible hand" only works—to the extent that the information processed by the markets is accurate and complete. *See* Joseph E. Stiglitz, *Globalization and Its Discontents* (2002) at ch. 3, n. 2 and accompanying text. On information asymmetry and the cost of capital, *see* Douglas Diamond and Robert Verrecchia, *Disclosure, Liquidity, and the Cost of Capital*, Journal of Finance, at 1325–1359 (Sept. 1991). *See also* S. P. Kothari, *The Role of Financial Reporting in Reducing Financial Risks in the Market*, in *Building and Infra*

structure for Financial Stability, at 89–102 (Eric. S. Rosengren and John S. Jordon eds., June 2000).

[12] *See id.* at 91.

[13] *See* James M. Landis, *The Legislative History of the Securities Act of 1933*, George Washington Law Review, at 30 (1959).

[14] *See* Chris Yenkey, *Transparency, Democracy, and the SEC: 70 Years of Securities Market Regulation, in Transparency in a New Global Order: Unvailing Organizational Visions* (Christina Garsten and Monica Lindh de Montoya eds., 2007).

[15] Peter S. Goodman, *The Reckoning: Taking Hard New Look at a Greenspan Legacy*, New York Times (Oct. 8, 2008).

[16] Henry Kaufman, *How the Credit Crisis Will Change the Way America Does Business: Huge Financial Companies Will Grow at the Expense of Borrowers and Investors*, Wall Street Journal (Dec. 6, 2008).

[17] *Central Bank of Denver, N.A. v. First Interstate Bank of Denver, N.A.*, 511 U.S. 164 (1994).

[18] *Stoneridge Investment Partners, LLC v. Scientific-Atlanta, Inc.*, 128 S. Ct. 761 (2008). *See also* Congressional Oversight Panel, Testimony of Joel Seligman, *Reforming America's Financial Regulatory Structure*, at 5 (Jan. 14, 2009) (online at cop.senate

[19] The Federal Reserve Board, *Remarks by Chairman Alan Greenspan before the Society of Business Economists, London, U.K.* (Sept. 25, 2002) (online at *www.federalreserve. gov/BoardDocs/Speeches/2002/200209252/default.htm).*

[20] *See* NFI, Gregory Elliehausen, *Consumers' Use of High-Price Credit Products: Do They Know What They Are Doing?*, at 29 (2006) (Working Paper No. 2006-WP-02); Credit Research Center, Georgetown University, Gregory Elliehausen and Edward C. Lawrence, *Payday Advance Credit in America: An Analysis of Customer Demand,* at 2 (2001) (online at www.cfsa.net/downloads/analysis_customer_demand.pdf).

[21] *See* Elliehausen, *supra* note 20, at 31.

[22] Senate Committee on Banking, Housing and Urban Affairs of the United States Senate, Testimony of Elizabeth Warren, *Examining the Billing, Marketing, and Disclosure Practices of the Credit Card Industry, and Their Impact on Consumers*, 110th Cong., at 1 (Jan. 25, 2007) (online at banking. The list of tricks and traps includes "universal default, default rates of interest, late fees, over-limit fees, fees for payment by telephone, repeated changes in the dates bills are due, changes in the locations to which bills should be mailed, making it hard to find the total amount due on the bill, moving bill- reception centers to lengthen the time it takes a bill to arrive by mail, misleading customers about grace periods, and double cycle billing." *Id.* at 3.

[23] Oren Bar-Gill and Elizabeth Warren, *Making Credit Safer*, University of Pennsylvania Law Review (Nov. 2008) (summarizing studies showing the high costs of consumer errors on checking accounts, credit cards, payday loans and refund anticipation loans).

[24] *See* Joint Economic Committee, *Sheltering Neighborhoods from the Subprime Foreclosure Storm*, at 15–16 (Apr. 2007) (online at jec.senate b61 f8a677c28) (hereinafter "JEC Report"). *See also* Nelson D. Schwartz, *Can the Mortgage Crisis Swallow a Town*?, New York Times (Sept. 2, 2007) (online at *www.nytimes. com/2007/09/02/ business/ yourmoney/02village.html);* U.S. Department of the Treasury, *Remarks by Secretary Henry M. Paulson, Jr. on Current Housing and Mortgage Market Developments at Georgetown University Law Center* (Oct. 16, 2007) (online at www.treasury.gov/press ("Foreclosures are costly and painful for homeowners. They are also costly for mortgage servicers and investors. They can have spillover effects into property values throughout a neighborhood, creating a downward cycle we must work to avoid.").

[25] JEC Report, *supra* note 24, at 17. *See also* Dan Immergluck and Geoff Smith, *The External Costs of Foreclosure: The Impact of Single-Family Mortgage Foreclosures on Property Values*, Housing Policy Debate, at 69–72 (2006) (finding that a single-family home foreclosure causes a decrease in values of homes within an eighth of a mile— or one city block—by an average of 0.9 percent, or approximately $1,870 when the average home sale

price is $164,599, and 1.44 percent in low- and moderate-income communities, or about $1,600 when the average home sale price is $111,002).

[26] *See, e.g.,* Desiree Hatcher, *Foreclosure Alternatives: A Case for Preserving Homeownership*, Profitwise News and Views, at 2 (Feb. 2006) (online at www.chicagofed.org/community

[27] *See* JEC Report, *supra* note 24, at 15.

[28] *See, e.g.,* Consumer Federation of America, Allan J. Fishbein and Patrick Woodall, *Exotic or Toxic? An Examination of the Non-Traditional Mortgage Market for Consumers and Lenders*, at 24 (May 2006) (online at www.consumerfed.org/ pdfs/Exotic_Toxic _Mortgage_Report0506.pdf); U.S. Department of Housing and Urban Development and U.S. Department of the Treasury, *Curbing Predatory Home Mortgage Lending,* at 35 (2000) (online at www.huduser.org/publications/ hsgfin/curbing.html); Center for Community Change, Bradford Calvin, *Risk or Race? Racial Disparities and the Subprime Refinance Market*, at 6–8 (May 2002) (online at butera-andrews.com/legislativeupdates/directory/ Background-Reports/Center%20for%20Community%20Change%20Report.pdf); Paul Calem, Kevin Gillen and Susan Wachter, *The Neighborhood Distribution of Subprime Mortgage Lending*, Journal of Real Estate Finance and Economics, at 401–404 (Dec. 2004). Another study, based on the Federal Reserve data, found that "African-American and Latino borrowers are at greater risk of receiving higher-rate loans than white borrowers, even after controlling for legitimate risk factors." Center for Responsible Lending, Debbie Gruenstein Bocian, Keith S. Ernst and Wei Li, *Unfair Lending: The Effect of Race and Ethnicity on the Price of Subprime Mortgages*, at 3 (May 31, 2006) (online at *www.responsiblelending. org/pdfs/rr011exec-Unfair_Lending-0506.pdf)*. A third study by the Survey Research Center at the University of Michigan found that black homeowners are significantly more likely to have prepayment penalties or balloon payments attached to their mortgages than nonblack homeowners, even after controlling for age, income, gender, and creditworthiness. Michael S. Barr, Jane K. Dokko, and Benjamin J. Keys, *Who Gets Lost in the Subprime Mortgage Fallout? Homeowners in Low- and Moderate-Income Neighborhoods* (Apr. 2008) (online at ssrn.com/abstract=1121215). And a fourth study, by Susan Woodward, found that black borrowers pay an additional $415 in mortgage fees and Latino borrowers pay an additional $365 in mortgage fees. Urban Institute, Susan Woodward, *A Study of Closing Costs for FHA Mortgages*, at ix (2008).

[29] Letter from Third Avenue Funds Chairman of the Board Martin J. Whitman to Shareholders, at 6 (Oct. 31, 2005) (online at www.thirdavenuefunds.com/ta/documents/sl/shareholderletters-05Q4.pdf).

[30] Abraham Lincoln, *Speeches and Writings, 1832–1858: Speeches, Letters, and Miscellaneous Writings,* at 301 (Don Edward Fehrenbacher ed., 1989).

[31] Franklin Roosevelt, *Remarks to the Commonwealth Club* (Sept. 23, 1932) (online at www.americanrhetoric.com/speeches/fdrcommonwealth.htm).

[32] Congressional Oversight Panel, Testimony of Joseph E. Stiglitz, *Reforming America's Financial Regulatory Structure*, at 3 (Jan. 14, 2009) (online at cop.senate

[33] Paul A. Volcker, *Address to the Economic Club of New York,* at 1-2 (Apr. 8, 2008) (online at econclubny.org/files/Transcript_Volcker_April_2008.pdf). In his address, Volcker recalled the financial troubles of New York City in 1975—that having been the last time he addressed the Economic Club of New York (then as President of the Federal Reserve Bank of New York). Volcker noted in his 2008 address, "Until the New York crisis, the country had been free from any sense of financial crisis for more than forty years." *Id.* at 1.

[34] *Id.* at 3.

[35] *See* Moss, *supra* note 3.

[36] Vesting that authority in an existing agency, such as the Board of Governors of the Federal Reserve, would require attention to the issues of transparency and accountability that the Panel will consider further when it looks at regulator structure.

[37] *See* Moss, *supra* note 3.

[38] Tobias Adrian and Hyun Song Shin, *Liquidity, Monetary Policy, and Financial Cycles*, Current Issues in Economics and Finance, at 1–7 (Jan./Feb. 2008). Some have argued that high leverage—especially short-term debt— may have a positive governance impact by imposing tough discipline on the management of financial institutions. K. Kashyap, Raghuram G. Rajan, and Jeremy Stein, *Rethinking Capital Regulation* (Aug. 2008) (online at www.kc.frb.org/publicat/sympos/2008/KashyapRajanStein.08.08.08.pdf) (paper prepared for Federal Reserve Bank of Kansas City symposium on "Maintaining Stability in a Changing Financial System" in Jackson Hole, Wyoming). Given the experiences of the last year, however, this theory requires a good deal more research.

[39] This illustration was inspired by: Brandeis University Rosenberg Institute of Global Finance and University of Chicago Initiative on Global Markets, David Greenlaw, et al., *Leveraged Losses: Lessons from the Mortgage Market Meltdown* (2008) (U.S. Monetary Forum Report No. 2) (online at research.chicagogsb.edu/igm/docs/USMPF_FINAL_Print.pdf); David Scharfstein, *Why Is the Crisis a Crisis* (Dec. 2, 2008) (slide presentation prepared for Colloquium on the Global Economic Crisis, Harvard Business School).

[40] Brookings Institute, Stephen Morris and Hyun Song Shin, *Financial Regulation in a System Context*, at 21– 26 (2008) (online at www.brookings.edu/economics _shin.pdf). *See also id.* at 23 ("Instead of risks on the asset side of the balance sheet, the focus is on the liabilities side of balance sheets, and the potential spillover effects that result when financial institutions withdraw funding from each other. Thus, it is raw assets, rather than risk-weighted assets that matter.").

[41] Federal Deposit Insurance Corporation, *Remarks by Sheila C. Bair, Chairman before the Conference on International Financial Instability: Cross-Border Banking and National Regulation, Federal Reserve Bank of Chicago and the International Association of Deposit Insurers* (Oct. 5, 2006) (online at *www.fdic.gov/news/ news/speeches/ archives/2006/ chairman/spoct0606.html).*

[42] *See, e.g., Spanish Steps: A Simple Way of Curbing Banks' Greed*, Economist (May 15, 2008) (online at www.economist.com/specialreports/displaystory.cfm?story_id

[43] House Financial Services Committee, Testimony of Joseph Stiglitz, *The Future of Financial Services Regulation*, 110th Cong. (Oct, 21, 2008) (online at financialservices. house.gov/hearing110/stiglitz102108.pdf). Stiglitz also notes that there are "several alternatives to speed limits imposed on the rate of expansion of assets: increased capital requirements, increased provisioning requirements, and/or increased premia on deposit insurance for banks that increase their lending (lending in any particular category) at an excessive rate can provide incentives to discourage such risky behavior." *Id.*

[44] Liquidity requirements can mitigate contagion, and can play a similar role to capital buffers in curtailing systemic failure. In some cases, liquidity may be more effective than capital buffers in forestalling systemic effects. When asset prices are extremely volatile, for example during periods of major financial distress, even a large capital buffer may be insufficient to prevent contagion, since the price impact of selling into a falling market would be very high. Liquidity requirements can mitigate the spillover to other market participants generated by the price impact of selling into a falling market. Moreover, because financial institutions do not recognise the indirect benefits of adequate liquidity holdings on other network members (and more generally on system resilience), their liquidity choices will be suboptimal. As a result, liquidity and capital requirements need to be imposed externally, in relation to a bank's contribution to systemic risk.

Bank of England, Rodrigo Cifuentes, Gianluigi Ferrucci, and Hyun Song Shin, *Liquidity Risk and Contagion* (2005) (Working Paper No. 264) (online at *www.bankofengland.co.uk/publications/workingpapers/wp264.pdf).* U.S. bank regulators monitor a bank's liquidity as part of their Uniform Financial Institutions Ratings (CAMELS) System. *See, e.g.,* Board of Governors of the Federal Reserve System, *Commercial Bank Examination Manual*, Sec. 2020.1.

[45] *See, e.g.*, Bill Gross, *Beware Our Shadow Banking System*, Fortune (Nov. 28, 2007) (online at money Nouriel Roubini, *The Shadow Banking System is Unraveling*, Financial Times (Sept. 21, 2008) (online at www.ft.com/cms/s/0/622acc9e-87f1-11dd-b114- 0000779fd1 8c.html).

[46] Off-balance sheet entities are a significant part of the shadow financial system, and are addressed in part in our earlier recommendations on leverage, and in part should be the subject of a more extended technical inquiry into reforming Financial Accounting Standard 140.

[47] In a speech on August 22, 2008, Federal Reserve Chairman Ben Bernanke spoke frankly about the potential for a Bear Stearns failure to echo throughout the financial system:

Although not an extraordinarily large company by many metrics, Bear Stearns was deeply involved in a number of critical markets, including (as I have noted) markets for short-term secured funding as well as those for over-the-counter (OTC) derivatives. One of our concerns was that the infrastructures of those markets and the risk- and liquidity-management practices of market participants would not be adequate to deal in an orderly way with the collapse of a major counterparty. With financial conditions already quite fragile, the sudden, unanticipated failure of Bear Stearns would have led to a sharp unwinding of positions in those markets that could have severely shaken the confidence of market participants. The company's failure could also have cast doubt on the financial conditions of some of Bear Stearns's many counterparties or of companies with similar businesses and funding practices, impairing the ability of those firms to meet their funding needs or to carry out normal transactions. As more firms lost access to funding, the vicious circle of forced selling, increased volatility, and higher haircuts and margin calls that was already well advanced at the time would likely have intensified. The broader economy could hardly have remained immune from such severe financial disruptions. Board of Governors of the Federal Reserve System, *Chairman Ben S. Bernanke Remarks on Reducing Systemic Risk before the Federal Reserve Bank of Kansas City's Annual Economic Symposium* (Aug. 22, 2008) (online at www.federalreserve.gov/newsevents/ speech/bernanke20080822a.htm).

[48] *See* President's Working Group on Financial Markets, *Policy Objectives for the OTC Derivatives Market* (Nov. 14, 2008) (online at www.treas.gov/press

[49] Christopher Cox, *Swapping Secrecy for Transparency*, New York Times (Oct. 18, 2008) (online at www.nytimes.com/2008/10/19/opinion/19cox.html).

[50] *See* Federal Reserve Board, Christopher J. Mayer, Karen M. Pence, and Shane M. Sherlund, *The Rise in Mortgage Defaults*, at 2 (2008) (Finance and Economics Discussion Series No. 2008-59) (online at www.federalreserve.gov/Pubs/feds/2008/200859/200859pap.pdf) ("According to data from the Mortgage Bankers Association, the share of mortgage loans that were 'seriously delinquent' (90 days or more past due or in the process of foreclosure) averaged 1.7 percent from 1979 to 2006... But by the second quarter of 2008, the share of seriously delinquent mortgages had surged to 4.5 percent."). For detailed historical data on prime and subprime mortgages, *see* Mortgage Bankers Association, *National Delinquency Survey* (online at *www.mbaa.org/ ResearchandForecasts/ productsandsurveys/ national delinquencysurvey.htm).*

[51] In 2002, for example, researchers at Citibank concluded that at least 40 percent of those who were sold high interest rate, subprime mortgages would have qualified for prime-rate loans. Lew Sichelman, *Community Group Claims CitiFinancial Still Predatory*, Origination News, at 25 (Jan. 2002) (reporting on new claims of CitiFinancial's predatory practices after settlements with state and federal regulators). Freddie Mac and Fannie Mae estimate that between 35 percent and 50 percent of borrowers in the subprime market could qualify for prime market loans. *See* James H. Carr & Lopa Kolluri, *Predatory Lending: An Overview*, in Fannie Mae Foundation, *Financial Services in Distressed Communities: Issues and Answers,* at 31, 37 (2001). *See also* Lauren E. Willis, *Decisionmaking and the Limits of Disclosure: The Problem of Predatory Lending: Price*, Maryland Law Review, at 730 (2006). A study by the Department of Housing and Urban Development of all mortgage

lenders revealed that 23.6 percent of middle-income families (and 16.4 percent of upper-income families) who refinanced a home mortgage ended up with a high-fee, high- interest subprime mortgage. U.S. Department of Housing and Urban Development, Randall M. Scheessele, *Black and White Disparities in Subprime Mortgage Refinance Lending*, at 28 (2002) (Working Paper No. HF-014) (online at *www.huduser.org/ Publications/ pdf/workpapr14.pdf*). A study conducted for the Wall Street Journal showed that from 2000 to 2006, 55 percent of subprime mortgages went to borrowers with credit scores that would have qualified them for lower-cost prime mortgages. Rick Brooks and Ruth Simon, *Subprime Debacle Traps Even the Very Credit Worthy; As Housing Boomed, Industry Push Loans to a Broader Market*, Wall Street Journal (Dec. 3, 2007) (study by First American Loan Performance for the Journal). By 2006, that proportion had increased to 61 percent. *Id.* None of these studies is definitive on the question of overpricing because they focus exclusively on FICO scores, which are critical to loan pricing but are not the only factor to be considered in credit risk assessment. However, they suggest significant market problems.

[52] Joint Center for Housing Studies, Harvard University, Ren S. Essene and William Apgar, *Understanding Mortgage Market Behavior: Creating Good Mortgage Options for All Americans*, at 2 (2007) (online at www.jchs.harvard.edu/publications/finance (quoting Fishbein and Woodall, *supra* note 28, at 24); Howard Lax, et al., *Subprime Lending: An Investigation of Economic Efficiency*, Housing Policy Debate, at 533 (2004).

[53] *See, e.g.*, Howell E. Jackson and Jeremy Berry, *Kickbacks or Compensation: The Case of Yield Spread Premiums* (Jan. 2002) (online at www.law. In some neighborhoods these brokers went door-to-door, acting as "bird dogs" for lenders, looking for unsuspecting homeowners who might be tempted by the promise of extra cash. Other families were broadsided by extra fees and hidden costs that didn't show up until it was too late to go to another lender. One industry expert described the phenomenon: "Mrs. Jones negotiates an 8% loan and the paperwork comes in at 10%. And the loan officer or the broker says, 'Don't worry, I'll take care of that, just sign here.'" Dennis Hevesi, *A Wider Loan Pool Draws More Sharks*, New York Times (Mar. 24, 2002).

[54] In any of these situations, of course, the state from which the financial institution switches its charter is deprived of substantial revenue, and the new chartering jurisdiction gains substantial revenue.

[55] Michael Schroeder, *Bank Regulator Cleans House*, Wall Street Journal (Aug. 19, 2005) ("Bank consolidation has created competition among regulators. The OCC has been a winner in wooing banks to choose it as their regulator, helping to keep its coffers flush. Bank fees finance its $519 million annual budget, not taxpayer money.").

[56] *See, e.g.*, Senate Committee on Banking, Housing, and Urban Affairs, Testimony of Arthur E. Wilmarth, Jr., *Review of the National Bank Preemption Rules,* 108th Cong. (Apr. 7, 2004) (online at banking Christopher L. Peterson, *Federalism and Predatory Lending: Unmasking the Deregulatory Agenda*, Temple Law Review, at 70–74, 77–84 (2005).

[57] Christopher L. Peterson, *Usury Laws, Payday Loans and Statutory Sleight of Hand: Salience Distortion in American Credit Pricing Limits*, Minnesota Law Review, at 1139 (2008).

[58] Greg Ip and Damian Palleta, *Regulators Scrutinized in Mortgage Meltdown*, Wall Street Journal (Mar. 27,

[59] *See, e.g., Watters v. Wachovia Bank*, 550 U.S. 1 (2007). *See also* Elizabeth R. Schiltz, *The Amazing, Elastic, Ever-Expanding Exportation Doctrine and Its Effect on Predatory Lending Regulation*, Minnesota Law Review (2004); Cathy Lesser Mansfield, *The Road to Subprime "HEL" Was Paved with Good Congressional Intentions: Usury Deregulation and the Subprime Home Equity Market*, South Carolina Law Review (2000).

[60] Truth in Lending Act (TILA), Pub. L. No. 90-321 (1968), at § 105(a) (codified as amended at 15 U.S.C. § 1601 et seq.) ("The Board shall prescribe regulations to carry out the purposes of this title."). The Federal Reserve Board implements TILA through its Regulation Z. 12 C.F.R. pt. 226. *See also* Home Ownership and Equity Protection Act of 1994 (HOEPA), Pub. L. No. 103-325 (codified at 15 U.S.C. § 1639) (amending TILA).

[61] Congress has amended TILA to improve consumer credit protection. *See, e.g.*, Fair Credit and Charge Card Disclosure Act of 1988, Pub. L. No. 100-583 (codified at 15 U.S.C. § 1637). In 1994, Congress amended TILA again to address predatory lending in the mortgage market. HOEPA, *supra* note 60.

[62] In 2007, Chairman Bernanke said the Board would "consider whether other lending practices meet the legal definition of unfair and deceptive and thus should be prohibited under HOEPA." Board of Governors of the Federal Reserve System, *Chairman Ben S. Bernanke Remarks on The Subprime Mortgage Market before the Federal Reserve Bank of Chicago's 43rd Annual Conference on Bank Structure and Competition* (May 17, 2007) (online at www.federalreserve.gov/newsevents/speech. In 2008, recognizing that its authority under HOEPA is "broad," the Board strengthened Regulation Z. 73 Fed. Reg. 44,522 (July 30, 2008).

[63] It was not until the end of 2001, after the volume of subprime loans had increased nearly 400 percent, that the Board restricted more abusive practices and broadened the scope of mortgages covered by HOEPA. *See* 66 Fed. Reg. 65,604, 65,605 (Dec. 20, 2001).

[64] The Fed updated Regulation Z in response to HOEPA in March 1995. 60 Fed. Reg. 15,463. It also amended Regulation C, "Home Mortgage Disclosure," in 2002. 67 Fed. Reg. 7222. Nonetheless, neither regulation was strong enough to head off the mortgage abuses that continued to accelerate through 2008.

[65] *See, e.g.*, Jane Birnbaum, *Credit Card Overhauls Seem Likely*, New York Times (July 5, 2008) ("Representative Barney Frank, Democrat of Massachusetts and chairman of the House Financial Services Committee, said the Federal Reserve acted last fall after the House approved legislation that would have transferred some of the Fed's regulatory power to other agencies. 'At that point, I said use it or lose it,' Mr. Frank recalled. 'And subsequent to that, the Fed began using its authority, and is now proposing rules similar to those in our credit card bill.'")

[66] House Financial Services Committee, Subcommittee on Financial Institutions and Consumer Credit, Statement of Chairman Barney Frank, *The Credit Cardholders' Bill of Rights: Providing New Protections for Consumers,* 110th Cong. 5–6 (2008).

[67] Steven Balsam, *An Introduction to Executive Compensation*, at 161 (2002).

[68] According to academic literature, between 1992 and 2002, the inflation-adjusted value of employee options granted by firms in the S&P 500 increased from an average of $22 million per company to $141 million per company, rising as high as $238 million per company in 2000. One academic study we referenced showed that, whereas in 1992 share options accounted for only 24 percent of the average pay package for these CEOs, by 2002 options comprised approximately half of the typical CEO's total compensation. The practice of granting option awards has not been limited to the top echelon of company executives. The percentage of option grants to all employees has grown steadily as well, if not at the same pace as the very top-most strata of corporate executives.

Senate Committee on Homeland Security and Governmental Affairs, Permanent Subcommittee on Investigations, Testimony of John W. White, *Concerning Tax and Accounting Issues Related to Employee Stock Option Compensation*, 110th Cong. (June 5, 2007) (online at idea.sec.gov/news/testimony (internal citations omitted).

[69] Jeanne Sahadi, *CEO Pay: Sky High Gets Even Higher*, CNNMoney.com (Aug. 30, 2005) (online at money

[70] *See, e.g.*, U.S. Securities Exchange Commission, *SEC Charges Former Apple General Counsel for Illegal Stock Option Backdating* (Apr. 24, 2007) (online at www.sec.gov/news/press

[71] The most prominent example is that of Angelo Mozilo, the former Chief Executive Officer of Countrywide Financial Corporation. Countrywide was rescued from bankruptcy by being acquired by Bank of America, which is now itself seeking additional financial assistance from the TARP. Mozilo realized more than $400 million in compensation from 2001 to 2007, most of it in the form of stock related compensation that he received and cashed out during the online. Similarly, three of Merrill Lynch's top executives realized a combined

$200 million in bonuses shortly before Bank of America absorbed that firm. Andrew Clark, *Banking Crisis: Merrill Lynch Top Brass Set to Share $200m*, The Guardian (Sept. 17, 2008) (online at www.guardian

[72] CFA Centre for Financial Market Integrity and the Business Roundtable Institute for Corporate Ethics, *Breaking the Short-Term Cycle: Discussion and Recommendations on How Corporate Leaders, Asset Managers, Investors, and Analysts Can Refocus on Long-Term Value*, at 9-10 (2006) (online at www.darden.virginia.edu/corporateethics/pdf/Short-term

[73] *Id.*

[74] Lucian Bebchuk and Jesse Fried, *Pay Without Performance: The Unfulfilled Promise of Executive Compensation*, 139 (2004).

[75] Federal Reserve Bank of St. Louis, William R. Emmons and Gregory E. Sierra, *Executive Compensation at Fannie Mae and Freddie Mac* (Oct. 26, 2004) (Working Paper No. 2004-06) (online at papers.ssrn.com/sol3/papers.cfm?abstract_id

[76] *Id.*

[77] Sarbanes-Oxley Act of 2002, Pub.L. No. 107-204, at § 304.

[78] Frank Bass and Rita Beamish, *Study: $1.6B of Bailout Funds Given to Bank Execs*, Associated Press (Dec. 21, 2008).

[79] Conference Board, Linda Barrington, Ellen S. Hexter, and Charles Mitchell, *CEO Challenge 2008: Top 10 Challenges—Financial Crisis Edition* (Nov. 2008) (online at www.conferenceboard.org/publications/describe.cfm?id

[80] Aspen Institute, *Long-Term Value Creation: Guiding Principles for Corporations and Investors* (2008).

[81] Harvard Business School, Joshua D. Coval, Jakib Jurek, and Erik Stafford, *The Economics of Structured Finance*, at 4 (2008) (Working Paper No. 09-060) (online at papers.ssrn.com/sol3/papers.cfm?abstract_id

[82] *Id.*

[83] Richard Cantor and Frank Packer, *The Credit Rating Industry*, FRBNY Quarterly Review, at 4 (Summer– Fall 1994). *See also* Claire Hill, *Regulating the Rating Agencies*, Washington University Law Quarterly, at 50 (2004).

[84] Cantor and Packer, *supra* note 81, at 4.

[85] House Committee on Oversight and Government Reform, Testimony of Jerome S. Fons, *Credit Rating Agencies and the Financial Crisis*, 110th Cong., at 3 (Oct. 22, 2008) (online at oversight

[86] John P. Hunt, *Credit Rating Agencies and the 'Worldwide Credit Crisis': The Limits of Reputation, the Insufficiency of Reform, and a Proposal for Improvement*, Columbia Business Law Review, at 32-33 (2009) (papers.ssrn. com/sol3/ papers.cfm?abstract_id

[87] Jeffrey David Manns, *Rating Risk after the Subprime Mortgage Crisis: A User Fee Approach for Rating Agency Accountability*, North Carolina Law Review (forthcoming), at 32–33 (papers.ssrn.com/sol3/papers.cfm?abstract_id (accessed Jan. 4, 2009).

[88] U.S. Securities and Exchange Commission Office of Compliance Inspections and Examinations, *Summary Report of Issues Identified in the Commission Staff's Examinations of Select Credit Rating Agencies,* at 33 (July 2008) (online at *www.sec.gov/ news/ studies/2008/craexamination070808.pdf)* (hereinafter "Summary Report") ("In addition to the recent growth in subprime origination, there has also been a growth in the risk factors associated with subprime mortgages. Studies indicate that the percentage of subprime loans with less-than-full documentation, high combined loan to total value (CLTVs), and second liens grew substantially between 1999 and 2006. Notably, while 2/28 adjustable rate mortgages comprised just 31 percent of subprime mortgages in 1999, they comprised almost 69 percent of subprime loans in 2006. Further, 40-year mortgages were virtually non-existent prior to 2005, but they made up almost 27 percent of the subprime loans in 2006. These data provide evidence that the majority of subprime origination occurred within the last five years, and the loans containing very high risk combinations are even more recent."). The SEC report also documented that, at one major credit rating agency,

"the average percentage of subprime RMBS in the collateral pools of CDOs it rated grew from 43.3 percent in 2003 to 71.3 percent in 2006." *Id.* at 7. Given these dramatic changes in the mortgage market, basing models on historical mortgage data may have proved particularly problematic.

[89] Indeed, a significant degree of independence was essential, since "CDOs rely on the power of diversification to achieve credit enhancement." Coval, et al., *supra* note 81, at 10.

[90] *See id.* at 23.

[91] *Id.* at 10.

[92] Credit Rating Agency Reform Act of 2006, Pub. L. No. 109-291.

[93] U.S. Securities Exchange Commission, *Nationally Recognized Statistical Rating Organizations* (online at www.sec.gov/divisions/marketreg/ratingagency.htm) (accessed Jan. 26, 2008) (hereinafter "SEC NRSRO Web site"). These ten include the old line firms Moody's, Standard & Poor's, and Fitch. *Id.*

[94] Senate Committee on Banking, Housing, and Urban Affairs, Testimony of Christopher Cox, *Turmoil in U.S. Credit Markets: The Role of the Credit Rating Agencies,* 110th Cong. (Apr. 22, 2008) (online at www.sec.gov/news/testimony

[95] SEC NRSRO Web site, *supra* note 93.

[96] House Committee on Oversight and Government Reform, Testimony of Sean J. Egan, *Credit Rating Agencies and the Financial Crisis*, 110th Cong., at 9 (Oct. 22, 2008) (online at oversight

[97] David G. Raboy, *Concept Paper on Credit Rating Agency Incentives* (Jan. 9, 2009) (unpublished working paper on file with the Panel).

[98] Hill, *supra* note 83, at 86–87.

[99] Egan, *supra* note 96, at 8.

[100] Senate Committee on Banking, Housing, and Urban Affairs, Testimony of Frank Partnoy, *Assessing the Current Oversight and Operation of Credit Rating Agencies,* 109th Cong., at 5 (Mar. 7, 2006) (online at banking

[101] A recent SEC report acknowledged, "The rating agencies' performance in rating these structured finance products raised questions about the accuracy of their credit ratings generally as well as the integrity of the ratings process as a whole." Summary Report, *supra* note 88, at 2).

[102] Frank Partnoy has suggested linking regulation instead to market-based measures of risk, such as credit spreads or the prices of credit default swaps. Partnoy, *supra* note 100, at 80–81.

[103] *See* Sarbanes-Oxley Act of 2002, Pub. L. No. 107-204, at §§ 101–109.

[104] Securities Industry Association, *Securities Industry Fact Book*, at 30 (2002) (online at www.sifma.org/research/statistics

[105] Steven Erlanger and Katrin Bennhold, *Governments on Both Sides of the Atlantic Push to Get Banks to Lend*, New York Times (Nov. 6, 2008).

[106] Senior Supervisors Group, *Observations on Risk Management Practices in the Recent Market Turbulence* (Mar. 6, 2008) (online at www.newyorkfed.org/newsevents/news/ banking

[107] *See, e.g., Meet Dr. Doom*, IMF Survey, at 308 (Oct. 16, 2006) (online at www.imf.org/EXTERNAL/PUBS/FT/SURVEY/2006/101606.pdf).

[108] *See, e.g., id.*

[109] Government Accountability Office, *Financial Regulation: A Framework for Crafting and Assessing Proposals to Modernize the Outdated U.S. Financial Regulatory System,* at 16–23 (2009). (online at www.gao.gov/new.items/d09216.pdf) (discussing overleveraging and financial interconnectedness as contributing to a risky financial environment immediately preceding the current crisis).

[110] *Id.*

[111] *Id.* at 18–19.

[112] *See, e.g.,* Nassim Nicholas Taleb, *The Black Swan: The Impact of the Highly Improbable* (2007); Daniel G. Goldstein and Nassim Nicholas Taleb, *We Don't Quite Know What We*

Are Talking About When We Talk About Volatility (Mar. 28, 2007) (online at ssrn.com/abstract=970480).

113 Even where outside advisory groups have been set up to counsel the Government regularly on economic issues, as the Conseil d'Analyse Economique (CAE) does in France, there is a marked similarity of backgrounds among their membership. Conseil d'Analyse Économique, *Membres du Conseil* (online at www.cae.premier-ministre.gouv.fr) (accessed Jan. 26, 2009). This may help explain why these bodies did not produce even minority viewpoints warning of the current financial crash; CAE did not produce a report on the subprime mortgage crisis until September, 2008. Conseil d'Analyse Économique, *Rapports du Conseil d'analyse économique* (online at www.cae.premier-ministre.gouv.fr) (accessed Jan. 26, 2009).

114 Timothy Curry and Lynn Shibut, *The Cost of the Savings and Loan Crisis: Truth and Consequences*, FDIC Banking Review (December 2000) (online at *www.fdic.gov/bank/ analytical/banking*

115 Tim Critchfield with Tyler Davis, Lee Davison, Heather Gratton, George Hanc, and Katherine Samolyk, *Community Banks: Their Recent Past, Current Performance, and Future Prospects* (2004) (online at www.fdic.gov/bank/analytical/future/fob_03.pdf) (hereinafter "FDIC Future of Banking Study").

116 John Kennedy, *Gov. Crist, State Regulators Reject State Farm's 7 Percent Rate Reduction*, Chicago Tribune (July 31, 2007) (online at www.chicagotribune.com/business/sfl-0731statefarm,0,3467689.story).

117 House Financial Services Committee, Subcommittee on Capital Markets, Securities, and Government Sponsored Enterprises, Testimony of Gary Gensler, *Securities and Government Sponsored Enterprises*, 106th Cong. (Mar. 22, 2000) (online at financialservices.house.gov/banking

118 David Leonhardt, *Washington's Invisible Hand*, New York Times (Sept. 26, 2008).

119 House Financial Services Committee, Oral Remarks of Alice Rivlin, *The Future of Financial Services*

120 *Bill v. Barack on Banks*, Wall Street Journal (Oct. 1, 2008) (online at 120 *Bill v. Barack on Banks*, Wall Street Journal (Oct. 1, 2008)

121 Risk-based Capital Standards: Advanced Capital Adequacy Framework – Basel II, 72 Fed. Reg. 69,288 (Dec. 7, 2007) (to be codified at 12 C.F.R. pts. 3, 208, 225, 325, 559, 560, 563, 567) (online at www.setonresourcecenter.com/register/2007/Dec/07/69288A.pdf).

122 Binyamin Appelbaum and Ellen Nakashima, *Banking Regulator Played Advocate Over Enforcer*, Washington Post (Nov. 23, 2008.) (online at www.washingtonpost.com/wp-dyn/content/article/2008/1 1/22/AR20081 1220221 3_pf.html).

123 Bernard Shull, *The Limits of Prudential Supervision: Economic Problems, Institutional Failure and Competence* (1993) (online at www.levy.org/download

124 Federal Reserve Board, *Open Market Operations* (online at www.federalreserve.gov/fomc/ fundsrate.htm) (accessed Jan. 26, 2009).

125 Mark Zandi, *Financial Shock: A 360° Look at the Subprime Mortgage Implosion, and How to Avoid the Next Financial Crisis* (2009).

126 Federal Reserve Bank of St. Louis, *Economic Research* (online at research.stlouisfed.org/ fred2/series

127 *Remarks of John B. Taylor at the Symposium of Housing, Housing Finance, and Monetary Policy sponsored by the Federal Reserve Bank of Kansas City in Jackson Hole, Wyoming* (Sept. 2007) (online at *www.kc.frb.org/PUBLICAT/ SYMPOS/2007/PDF/ Taylor_ 0415. pdf*).

128 David Leonhardt and Vikas Bajaj, *Drop Foreseen in Median Price of U.S. Homes*, New York Times (Aug. 26, 2007) (online at www.nytimes.com/2007/08/26/business/26housing.html? ei=5090&en=9bd44f2f8b0ef4f4&ex=1345780800&partner=rs suserland&emc=rss&pagewanted=all).

[129] Zandi, *supra* note 125; Robert J. Shiller, *The Subprime Solution: How Today's Global Financial Crisis Happened, and What to Do About It* (2008).
[130] Robert B. Avery, Kenneth P. Brevoort, and Glenn B. Canner, *The 2006 HMDA Data*, Federal Reserve Bulletin (Dec. 2007).
[131] Taylor, *supra* note 127.
[132] U.S. Department of the Treasury, *The Community Reinvestment Act after Financial Modernization: A Baseline Report* (Apr. 2000).
[133] First Union Capital Markets Corp., *Bear, Stearns & Co. Price Securities Offering Backed By Affordable Mortgages Unique Transaction to Benefit Underserved Housing Market* (Oct. 20, 1997).
[134] *Fannie Mae Increase CRA Options*, ABA Banking Journal (Nov. 1, 2000).
[135] Boston Federal Reserve, *Closing the Gap: A Guide to Equal Opportunity Lending* (Apr. 1993) (online at www.bos.frb.org/commdev/commaff/closingt.pdf).
[136] Dale Westhoff, *Packaging CRA Loans into Securities*, Mortgage Banking (May 1, 1998) (online at www.allbusiness.com/personal-finance–1.html).
[137] U.S. Department of the Treasury, *Remarks of Assistant Secretary for Financial Institutions Emil W. Henry Jr., before the Housing Policy Council of the Financial Services Roundtable* (June 26, 2006) (online at www.ustreas.gov/press
[138] Russell Roberts, *How Government Stoked the Mania*, Wall Street Journal (Oct. 3, 2008).
[139] *Id.*
[140] *Id.*
[141] *Id.*
[142] Steven A. Holmes, *Fannie Mae Eases Credit to Aid Mortgage Lending*, New York Times (Sept. 30, 1999).
[143] Roberts, *supra* note 138.
[144] American Enterprise Institute, Peter Wallison and Charles Calomiris, *The Last Trillion-Dollar Commitment: The Destruction of Fannie Mae and Freddie Mac* (Sept. 30, 2008).
[145] Joint Center for Housing Studies, *The State of the Nation's Housing* (2008) (online at www.jchs.harvard.edu/publications/markets
[146] Charles Duhigg, *Pressured to Take More Risk, Fannie Reached Tipping Point*, New York Times (Oct. 5, 2008).
[147] *Fannie Mae Relaxes Loan Down Payment Requirements*, Reuters News Service (May 19, 2008).
[148] James R. Hagerty, *Fannie, Freddie Share Spotlight in Mortgage Mess*, Wall Street Journal (Oct. 16, 2008).
[149] Tom Raum and Jim Drinkard, *Fannie Mae, Freddie Mac Spent Millions on Lobbying*, Associated Press (July 17, 2008).
[150] Wallison and Calomiris, *supra* note 144.
[151] *Fannie Mae, Freddie Mac Spent Millions on Lobbying*, Associated Press (July 17, 2008).
[152] House Financial Services Committee, Statement of Rep. Richard Baker, *Joint Hearing on Government Sponsored Enterprises*, 105th Cong. (July 16, 1997) (online at financials ervices.house.gov/banking
[153] House Financial Services Committee, Subcommittee on Capital Markets, Securities, and Government Sponsored Enterprises, Statement of Rep. Richard Baker, *Housing GSE Regulatory Reform Hearing*, 106th Cong. (March 22, 2000) (online at financialservices.house.gov/banking
[154] House Financial Services Committee, *Archived Hearings* (online at *http://financial services. house.gov/archive_hearings.html).*
[155] H.R. 1461, 109th Cong. (2005)
[156] House Financial Services Committee, Subcommittee on Capital Markets, Securities, and Government Sponsored Enterprises, Testimony of Jim Bothwell of the Government Accountability Office, *Joint Hearing on Government Sponsored Enterprises*, 105th Cong. (July 16, 1997) (online at financialservices.house.gov/banking

[157] Gensler, *supra* note 117.

[158] Senate Committee on Banking, Housing, and Urban Affairs, Testimony of Alan Greenspan, *Proposals for Improving the Regulation of the Housing Government Sponsored Enterprises*, 108th Cong. (Feb. 24, 2004) (online at www.access.gpo.gov/congress

[159] House Financial Services Committee, Subcommittee on Capital Markets, Securities, and Government Sponsored Enterprises, Testimony of John Taylor, *Hearing on Improving Regulation of Housing GSEs*, 106th Cong. (June 15, 2000) (online at financial services.house.gov/banking

[160] House Financial Services Committee, Subcommittee on Capital Markets, Securities, and Government Sponsored Enterprises, Testimony of Bruce Marks, *Hearing on Improving Regulation of Housing GSEs*, 106th Cong. (June 21, 2000) (online at financial services.house.gov/banking

[161] House Financial Services Committee, Subcommittee on Capital Markets, Securities, and Government Sponsored Enterprises, Testimony of J. Timothy Howard of Fannie Mae, *Hearing on Reforming Fannie Mae and Freddie Mac*, 107th Cong. (July 11, 2001) (online at financialservices.house.gov/media

[162] House Financial Services Committee, Subcommittee on Capital Markets, Securities, and Government Sponsored Enterprises, Testimony of Mitchell Delk of Freddie Mac, *Hearing on Reforming Fannie Mae and Freddie Mac*, 107th Cong. (July 11, 2001) (online at financialservices.house.gov/media

[163] House Financial Services Committee, Oral remarks of Rep. Barney Frank, *Hearing on H.R. 2575, The Secondary Mortgage Market Enterprises Regulatory Improvement Act*, 108th Cong. (Sept. 25, 2003) (online at financialservices.house.gov/media

[164] *What They Said About Fan and Fred*, Wall Street Journal (Oct. 2, 2008).

[165] *Id.*

[166] House Financial Services Committee, Statement of Rep. Maxine Waters, *Hearing on Housing Government Sponsored Enterprises*, 107th Cong. (July 16, 2002) (online at financial services.house.gov/media

[167] House Committee on Oversight and Government Reform, *Hearing on Credit Rating Agencies and the Financial Crisis*, 110th Cong. (Oct. 22, 2008) (online at oversight

[168] AEI Center for Regulatory and Market Studies, Lawrence J. White, *Lessons from the Debacle of '07- '08 for Financial Regulation and Its Overhaul* (Jan. 2009) (Working Paper No. 09-0 1).

[169] Financial Crimes Enforcement Network, *FinCEN Assessment Reveals Suspected Mortgage Loan Fraud Continues to Rise* (Nov. 3, 2007).

[170] Richard B. Schmitt, *FBI Saw Threat of Loan Crisis,* Los Angeles Times (Aug. 25, 2008).

[171] *Id.*

[172] Stephen Labaton, *Agency's '04 Rule Let Banks Pile on New Debt,* New York Times (Oct. 2, 2008).

[173] Edward L. Glaeser, *Better, Not Just More, Regulation*, Economix (Oct. 28, 2008) (available at economix.blogs).

[174] *Blame Fannie Mae and Congress for the Credit Mess*, Wall Street Journal (Sept. 23, 2008).

[175] Peter Wallison, *Regulating Fannie Mae and Freddie Mac* (May 13, 2005) (online at www.aei.org/publications/pubID.22514/pub_detail.asp).

[176] The Group of 30, *Financial Reform: A Framework for Financial Stability* (Jan. 15, 2009) (online at www.group30.org/pubs/recommendations.pdf).

[177] The Committee on Capital Markets Regulation, *Recommendations for Reorganizing the U.S. Financial Regulatory Structure* (Jan. 14, 2009) (online at *www.capmktsreg. org/ pdfs/ CCMR%20-* %20Recommendations%20for%20Reorganizing%20the%20US%20Regulatory%20Structur e.pdf).

[178] U.S. Department of Treasury, *Blueprint for a Modernized Financial Regulatory Structure* (Mar. 31, 2008) (online at www.ustreas.gov/press (hereinafter "Blueprint").

[179] Walter W. Eubanks , U.S. Congressional Research Service, RL33 036, , *Federal Financial Services Regulatory Consolidation: An Overview* (July 10, 2008), at 14.

[180] Government Accountability Office, *U.S. and Foreign Experience May Offer Lessons for Modernizing U.S. Structure* (Nov. 1996) (online at *www.gao.gov/ archive/1997/ gg97023.pdf).*

[181] Blueprint, *supra* note 178.

[182] *Id.*

[183] Seligman, *supra* note 18.

[184] House Financial Services Committee, Subcommittee on Capital Markets, Securities, and Government Sponsored Enterprises, Testimony of Rep. Sue Kelly, *NARAB & Beyond: Achieving Nationwide Uniformity in Agent Licensing*, 107th Cong. (May 16, 2001) (online at financialservices.house.gov/media

[185] John Sununu, et al., *Insurance Companies Need a Federal Regulator*, Wall Street Journal (Sept. 23, 2008) (online at online.wsj.com/article/SB122212967854565511.html).

[186] Omnibus Reconciliation Act of 1993, Pub. L. No. 103-66, at § 13211.

Chapter Sources

The following chapters have been previously published:

Chapter 1 – These remarks were delivered as Statement of Gene L. Dodaro, Acting Comptroller General of the United States, before the Committee on Banking, Housing and Urban Affairs, U.S. Senate, dated February 4, 2009.

Chapter 2 – This is an edited, excerpted and augmented edition of a Congressional Oversight Panel Special Report on Regulartory Reform, dated January 2009.

INDEX

B

C

D

G

H

J

K

L

M

Q

R

S

T